MW01258243

The

Kundalini

Guide

A COMPANION FOR THE

INWARD JOURNEY

Volume 1: ENERGY

By

Bonnie L. Greenwell Ph.D.

Copyright 2014 by Bonnie Greenwell

All rights reserved

Please do not reproduce or copy any portion of this book either electronically or in print without the written permission of the author, with the exception of brief quotes embedded in reviews.

She may be contacted through her websites:
www.kundaliniguide.com or www.awakeningguide.com

Published by Shakti River Press, Ashland, OR
Contact: shantiriver@gmail.com

Cover Art:
Tontyn Hopman of Zurich, Switzerland

Cover Design:
Deborah Perdue: www.illuminationgraphics.com

ISBN-10: 0-9627327-2-9

ISBN-13: 978-0-9627327-2-0

DEDICATION

This book is dedicated to all the people who have shared
their stories of spiritual awakening with me over the past
30 years, in hopes it will support all those in the future
who will enter the mystery of these experiences. It is
offered with loving appreciation to my mentor and teacher,
Adyashanti, who helped bring this experience to fruition in
my life and in many others.

Table of Contents

Introduction

An intense energy spasm suddenly rolled up my spine and through my head. My body jerked upright as rivulets of bliss moved through my nervous system. It was like being electrified with joy. With the persistence of labor pains the energies pushed upward over and over, each roll more intense than the one before, my mind becoming progressively less focused. After a few minutes I was barely present in the room where I was sitting, listening to a college lecture on developmental psychology. I did not know it then but the direction of my life, my interests and my work was being blasted into new territory, and I would never again see the world through the same lens. Something powerful had grabbed me and turned me in a new direction.

When the class was over I stumbled down the hall and into a small meditation room at the Institute of Transpersonal Psychology, where I was a graduate student. I sat on a cushion leaning against a wall and fell into a vast and open sense of spaciousness, my mind empty and quiet, my body completely lost in floating pleasure. Eventually I came back into my senses, but for weeks following I was in a state of awareness that was untouched by the normal challenges of my family, studies and work, even though they continued as usual. Walking down the street felt like floating, Waking in the morning felt like entering a new adventure. Sitting to meditate felt like falling into a world of light and bliss. At night my body would awake and shake itself, move into positions that stretched the spine, plunge my nervous system into a vibration of happiness, and occasionally produce an other-worldly dream.

During these weeks I needed to decide on a topic for my doctoral research, and since I was aware that what happened to me was called kundalini awakening in the culture of Indian yoga, I chose this subject for my research. I talked with a few others who had experienced similar awakenings, and discovered that for some it was not a pleasant experience, but instead it was painful, disturbing and frightening. I wanted to know why. What was the difference between a positive or challenging awakening? I decided to read everything written on the subject, which in 1986 was not much, and I entered the second phase of my professional life as a psychotherapist specializing in spiritual emergence. The dissertation morphed into the book "Energies of Transformation: A Guide to the Kundalini Process" in 1990, and led me to meet and consult with several thousand people over the next 25 years who had experienced some variation of this awakening.

This book condenses all I have learned over

these years, through the continuation and shifts of my own experience and the reports of the many people who shared their unique stories with me. It is a guide for those who will awaken through spiritual or devotional practice, near-death experience, energy or body therapies, trauma or drug use, or for reasons unknown, spontaneously. The purpose is to offer support, encouragement and understanding to those in this experience, and to help them move out of struggle and into peace, so they may enjoy the freedom of their true nature. It is dedicated with profound gratitude to everyone who ever told me his or her own story of awakening.

God, Consciousness and Energy

There is ample evidence that over many centuries and in many cultures methods have evolved in response to the needs of spiritual seekers who have wanted to know directly whether or not there is a God, or lacking the image or belief in "God" perhaps they asked simply, "Who or what am I, beyond this human mind and body?" Many of these practices have revealed a surprising connection between energy and consciousness, and demonstrated that the answer to our deepest questions comes from an interior experience.

When we answer the inward call to understand the nature of our lives, and to find answers for our deepest questions, we begin a journey into the depths and the source of consciousness. We may think we are seeking a vague destination we have heard described as self-realization, or enlightenment, a state of being the mind can only attempt to imagine but never truly grasp, but in fact we are inviting a ground-level change of identity. Some people embark on pilgrimages in search of wisdom. They may be ripened by exposure to the energy fields of sacred spaces, but ultimately the Truth can only be discovered by those who are inward bound, for we hold within us the answer to our own questions.

As with any journey we can read the maps created by others who have gone in this direction, we can prepare ourselves to leave home, and we can make our way using any number of vehicles – meditation, silence, transmission from a teacher, energy practices, prayer, sound, breathing practices, devotion, and numerous others. In some cases, the journey is initiated through a crisis or near-death trauma, a powerful emotional event, overwhelming love or passion, and even spontaneously without any obvious cause, and a person does not remember having asked for it.

There are stages that appear along the way of this passage into self understanding and peace, but they are not predictable or linear, for they appear with the unexpected quality of the journey taken by Alice in Wonderland, with strange events and openings happening unexpectedly, and about which we can feel puzzled, distracted, or even discouraged from continuing. This is a journey that can be ecstatic, stressful, astonishing, emotional, detached, joyful and chaotic all at once. It is never what one expects it to be, and no two people navigate it in exactly the same style. It is an adventure as variable as the lives we have lived.

One of the radical surprises in the spiritual process is the fact that it begins to impact the energy in our bodies. We are seldom advised that participation in energy practices or meditation, or even intense devotion and prayer, subtly begins to change the energy flows and the chemistry within us. These bio-energetic changes are an essential part of the preparation for a new sense of who we are, a new kind of consciousness. We may begin meditation practice seeking inner calm and peace, but as we enter our deepest stillness we may discover an awakening of energy beyond our imagination.

All of us have contractions and limitations in our self-expression because of energetic patterns locked into our bodies from the very beginning of life, woven through us as we were conditioned to feel and think in specific ways, to defend ourselves when we felt threatened, and to adapt and fit into our families, cultures and societies. At a deeper level the DNA likely holds familial and cultural patterning and certain other inherent tendencies. All of these experiences, as well as our capacity for sensation, intelligence, emotion and intuition, form an energy flow within us that is called the subtle body, or the energy body, in yoga science.

Imagine this subtle body to be like an energy grid made manifest by consciousness, through which is flowing every part of you that is not physical but invisible. It is the movement through which your senses communicate with thought, your mind connects with emotion, and memory, beliefs, desires, and knowledge accumulates and directs the tendencies of your life. Without this energy flow the body is simply a lifeless shell, as is obvious whenever you see a corpse. It is clear something has left the body. What left was the subtle energy field, the life force, the consciousness that is prior to your conditioned separate self.

There is a complex and ancient system that comes out of India, in which the entire schema of the subtle body field is described. Many people are familiar with the teachings about six or seven chakras (depending on the system), which are major energy vortexes of the subtle body, said to be junctures where physical, subtle and causal bodies intersect (the causal being an aspect of consciousness without form.) There are many other elements to this system, including thousands of *nadis* (lines of energy), other less known chakras, areas that are considered to be knotted, and other esoteric points. The idea is that during conception consciousness enters the egg through the sperm, sets in motion the development of the fetus, and activates the energy flow of the subtle field. When the subtle field is established the residual energy of consciousness coils at the base of the spine 3 ½ times. This holding energy is called kundalini, which is a Sanscrit word based on the term *kunda*, that means coiled.

Many practices in yoga and tantra are designed specifically to calm the body, and open the *nadis*, and bring attention to this coiled *kundalini*, releasing it up through the body, amplifying the energy field, and preparing the subtle system for self-realization. Along the way, this energy will work on blockages, charge cells, increase heat and energy, and open up areas that have been contracted. This is experienced as vibration, shaking, involuntary movements, heat and cold rushes, and other interior sensations. When this happens, it is called kundalini awakening. Other eastern systems recognize this activation of energy but call it by different terms. In China it is a chi crisis or Qigong crisis when this energy awakens, and it would not necessarily be considered a spiritual event, but one that leads ultimately to harmony, strength, improved health and greater awareness. There is evidence that the activation has been encouraged for various reasons and was a valued aspect of many indigenous cultures including Native American, Hawaiian, Egyptian, Peruvian, Tibetan, and African.

In its ordinary form, as energy flowing in the body, the terms prana (Indian), chi or Qi (Chinese) and ki (Japanese) are commonly understood in their respective traditions and are part of the ancient systems of medicine, which included methods for balancing and harmonizing it. In the West some researchers of this topic call this bio-energy, but it is little known or understood in mainstream western science and medicine, so most doctors will not be able to identify it or discuss it.

The activation of kundalini energy has been embraced by some schools of yoga in the West, and often marketed as a way to enhance health and longevity. But its true function is to shift a person's consciousness, to awaken his or her true nature, and it does this through a process that brings a deconstruction of the old self and collapses the familiar identifications. It may happen that health and longevity is improved but this is not a guarantee. Even people who are completely enlightened can experience physical pain and disease, and eventually pass away. Each of us will have our own unique experience with this energy, just as we do in other aspects of our lives.

This is a journey to freedom, and along the way there can be many joys and unexpected gifts. But it is perilous for the little "me", the personality that thinks life is about acquiring more and more for itself. This is not a reflection on the value of having a healthy personality, or a strong sense of personal direction in one's life. These are both useful goals from a human perspective, bringing satisfaction and creating roles in our society, and they are part of the nature of human creation. But when you have plowed the ground of your human conditioning many times, and found still there is something lacking, some inherent happiness you sense is available but cannot find, then you are ready for this inward journey to freedom.

This book is the first of two volumes reflecting the conditions you are likely to discover along the path to freedom: the pleasures, the territory, the cul-de-sacs and the potential outcome. It offers guidance accumulated through 25 years of listening to the reports of over two thousand people who have awakened kundalini. A companion volume, "The Awakening Guide", is also available that reflects upon other aspects of spiritual awakening from a non-dual perspective. Kundalini awakening is not the whole story of spiritual awakening, but only a stage, considered a method by some systems and a by-product by others. Because it has a great impact on the lives of many spiritual seekers, the intention of this book is to provide simple clarity about what is happening, and reveal how kundalini energy can be met in a way that best supports the spiritual journey.

Most people begin the passage to spiritual awakening because they feel driven to it. It seems that life will have no purpose or sense of completion until this is done. In addition to a sense of lack, they may be driven by their suffering, or by curiosity, or by a longing for knowledge, God or peace. It is as if some deep secret source within compels them to become seekers and then, along the way, to dissolve the one who seeks. This is an ancient passage, as old as recorded history, and as universal as any other human hunger. It is not a mainstream path, because most lives are content to live within the framework of a cultural and personal belief system, and so this journey is rarely recognized or supported by the consensus societies in which we live.

But those who have found fulfillment in this passage have always left pointers along the way that can lead other sincere seekers into Truth. We see this in the great images left in Indian caves and sculptures nearly 2000 years ago by early Buddhists,

Jains and Hindus. We see it in the ancient scriptures of India, and the treasured energy practices of China. Evidence of this may also be found in traditions as diverse as Chinese Taoism, Islamic Sufi teachings, Greek and Egyptian mystery schools, the Hawaiian Huna tradition, African and South American shamanic practices, and the rituals of some Native American Indian tribes. People have long sought a personal relationship with the Absolute, however they define it, and pursued an inward turning for Self-discovery.

In the West, many people are finding their own unique paths to awakening and wholeness. Hopefully these volumes will offer you the courage and the support you need to trust the power of the awakening process, and discover who you are. It is not such a dramatic leap, into the Now, into the Self, for it has always been here waiting for your spirit to remember and return. When kundalini awakens, the journey has become inevitable, as long as you understand the value of staying on the path.

With Deep Appreciation

I am indebted to many amazing people in my own spiritual and professional journey, and especially to my last teacher, Adyashanti, a man of remarkable natural wisdom and love. Many people have touched my life over the past 50 years with a spiritual teaching, a practice, or a pointer that kept me going in the right direction. These include Amelia Rathbun, a colorful and extraordinary teacher who wanted to change the world back in the 60's. Through an organization she founded called

Creative Initiative Foundation she introduced me to true spiritual seeking, and took away any idea I had that being a woman was a limitation. I also greatly honor a friend I ran into in the market back in 1967 who said I should read a remarkable book, "Autobiography of a Yogi" , and changed my life. Thank you to Thomas Parker, my Jungian analyst, who loved Paramahansa Yogananda, introduced me to Kriya Yoga, and told me to think with my belly. With his wife Harriet, and a small group, I traveled to sacred sites in Egypt and India, where I came to realize anything was possible.

Other gifts in my journey include a visit with Muktananda in the 1970's, who opened his pink Ashram in Oakland to everyone and who I visited when I was too young to know what I was doing; and some valued time with Gangaji, who demonstrated how an American woman can be alive and awake, and once stopped my mind with a single word. I owe much of the wonder in my life to Dr. Gay Hendricks, who showed me the connection between body and God, and awakened my slumbering energies through Radiance Breathwork.

I was blessed with wise teachers and caring friends at the Institute of Transpersonal Psychology who supported my kundalini awakening and my thesis work. Stan Grof, a visionary pioneer in breathwork, taught me about energy release, and offered brilliant explanations for many anomalous experiences. Dr. Joan Harrigan and her teacher Swami Chandrashekharananda hosted me in India, and gave me a good understanding of the classical

perspective of kundalini science from the Tamil
tradition. Baba Hari Dass of Mt. Madonna, gave me
access to his teachings about kundalini in the
Ashtanga Yoga tradition. Judith, Marea, Olga, Megan
(Maitreya), Maggie, Connie, Briget, Jonathan, Cherla,
and Ray are all dear friends who could talk with me
about the deepest insights and experiences and
helped to hone my ability to express myself. There
were many other great people who helped me to
found the Kundalini Research Network, which
expanded my work internationally and stimulated my
mind and creative expression. I am grateful to my
husband Bill, who always supported me through
these explorations and travels. And finally, my
education would have been incomplete without
Adyashanti, his wife Mukti, and his sangha
community, who put it all together for me with love,
and showed me new aspects of spiritual awakening.
Beyond this I am grateful for over 30 years of meeting
with people in spiritual process who had the courage
to share their experiences and move forward. Each
offered another valuable step in understanding.

None of us really know how deeply we may
influence the lives of others by simply being real and
available. It can seem as if we awaken alone, and
only realize something within us that was already
there, but there are numerous nudges that make this
possible. My deepest hope is that these guides will be
among those nudges for you, giving you the courage
to keep going until you remember you are free.

Chapter 1: What is Kundalini?

The eruption of kundalini energy from its secret nest at the base of the spine has been revered by some as bringing ecstasy and enlightenment, and disparaged by others as simply disabling, terrifying and dangerous. Mystics may call it a method of transformation. Skeptics consider it imaginary. Few who have not experienced it believe in its existence. All who have experienced it know it as a mystery and a profound life-altering experience.

The subtle energies that begin to move and vibrate within someone who feels the arising of kundalini, have been reported in many cultures over the centuries, but few in the west know of their power, and even fewer who have heard of it consider it real. This general lack of understanding intensifies its mystery and leaves many who awaken the energy stranded because their medical, spiritual, and energy advisors or guides are unable to comprehend the radical changes that kundalini stimulates in the subtle, psychological and physical systems of those who experience it. This is unfortunate, because anyone is vulnerable to this awakening, either as a result of practices or as a spontaneous event.

The Symbolism of Kundalini

Kundalini energy has been represented primarily by two symbols in ancient teachings, the most common being the serpent, because the energy is believed to be coiled at the base of the spine, until it shoots up like a cobra or twists inside a body as it awakens. This energy movement also triggers the shedding of the old identifications, just as the snake sheds its skin. The snake has long been a symbol for healing and the transformation of consciousness. Even the snake in the Garden of Eden could be interpreted as representing the transformation of consciousness, although in this case moving from the innocence of being a species identified with nature, and unaware of time, space, life and death, to the complications of becoming a human identified with the thoughts, beliefs and concerns of the human mind. A kundalini rising begins the process of reversing this journey, returning a person from mental complexity back to knowing Oneness, and returning with wisdom and understanding about existence rather than innocence.

Kundalini has also been imaged as a goddess, because feminine energy is most often associated with the birth and sustenance of life forms. She is an aspect of Shakti, who when awakened from her slumber at the base of the spine, rushes through the subtle body to be reunited above the crown of the head with her lover, Siva, who represents pure consciousness existing prior to, or without, form. She has been praised as a source of ecstasy and wisdom, and condemned as a cause of psychological disintegration, sought after for magical powers and longevity, and feared for her capacity to annihilate the mind. And yet the truth of this energy is that it is simply a term for the life force that animates all transient and living forms. Prana, chi or ki are the energies flowing within us that transfer thoughts, feeling, intelligence, sensation, connection and movement. Kundalini is their source, that which curls at the base of the spine and holds the system in stasis until it is activated or until it exits the body at death.

Kundalini As Consciousness

In the Vedanta science of India, as in many other wisdom traditions, it is understood that there is only One source of consciousness, which creates out of itself all forms that appear in existence, and we humans are part of this process. Consider that the consciousness inhabiting your body activated mysteriously through an energy flow initiated by this One consciousness during conception. Yogis believe this consciousness moves through sperm into the ovum, and this activates the growth of the fetus, which is eventually birthed as a human being. By the time we function as a human, this speck of pure consciousness is housed inside our cells and subtle body field, and its light is what looks through our eyes and moves through our senses, and is basically the energetic force of our lives. Everything that appears as living creation emanates in a similar way from this same consciousness.

Kundalini is a Sanscrit term for this energy of creation, the life force that causes consciousness to function in a body. After kundalini activates and enlivens a human body, the stabilized and consistent flow of internal energy that remains is known as prana in the scriptures of India. Breathing supports the flow of prana in living systems and is essential to the connection between spirit and body. Breathing practices taught in yoga and in other eastern energy-based traditions are effective in harmonizing, amplifying or redirecting prana to improve health and vitality, and in specialized training these flows are manipulated to cause a kundalini awakening.

Anyone can easily be trained to feel prana consciously, and people who do healing, practice Aikido or QiGong or other martial arts, or who are just highly sensitive, can feel it moving from their own hands, or sense it in someone else. In Indian medicine, prana is considered responsible for the flowing of energy in the body that causes everything from breathing to burping, swallowing to elimination, blinking to sneezing, the circulation of the heart and blood, and operating all other moving functions. The movement of senses, thoughts and emotions is carried by prana, and these actions form an entire flow of energies known as the subtle energy body. The efficiency with which this prana flows in a body has a significant impact on energy, spirit and health.

After setting the pranic field in motion, the residual kundalini energy coils at the base of the spine, holding the energy in stasis until we die, when it uncoils and leaves the body. This phenomenon would be irrelevant in your life, something you might take for granted the way you take for granted your heart beating and your digestive system working, except that under the right circumstances it can uncoil and force you into a radical systemic change that is part of the awakening.

Initial Awakenings

When kundalini energy is activated there is a great intensification of the life force. For a lifetime, this energy has been coiled at the base of the spine, having done its primary job of creating and stabilizing a life (you), but now it leaps into a new service. This time the work it does is to help you remember yourself as the source, as the pure consciousness that existed before you became identified as a separate self.

Kundalini awakening usually begins with a rush of energy up the spine or from the feet, and it may flow out of the head, but more often it stops at the heart or throat. It may come in spurts, as if a water hose is turning it on and off, jerking you upward with each shot of water. It may come smoothly and slowly, and feel as if it is winding through you like a snake. It may rush up violently, as if in a panic to get out, and feel like a huge wave of heat or pressure, leaving you terrified for your life.

A few rare people are plunged into cosmic consciousness at the first arising of kundalini energy. But more often it begins as a shaking or vibrating that may feel either gentle or harsh, perhaps bringing fear or perhaps bringing bliss, or even both at once. Sometimes it seems to hit one hard in the gut, or cause an eruption in the heart, or gagging in the throat. It can feel like a rush of sexual energy, or a whole-body orgasm. It can feel like flashes of light or heat. Whatever it does, you notice something unfamiliar is happening to you, and if you have never heard of the connection between energy and spirituality you are likely to be alarmed.

When you have had an awakening of kundalini energy in which it rises above the heart, you are launched on the interior journey. It may be a very slow trip, and there may be many detours and distractions along the way, but if you consciously choose to be among the inward bound, to seek within yourself for Truth or freedom, it will move more smoothly for you. To the extent you want to carry all the emotional luggage of your life along with you, it will have more challenges, just as any trip is made more stressful by a carrying along a ton of luggage. It will help greatly if you have an understanding of this process of kundalini awakening, just as any journey is made more smooth when you have a map, and more informative when you have a guidebook.

It may not seem fair that we cannot take everything we love with us on the spiritual path, but anyone who has tried to backpack up a mountain path knows the advantage of holding down the contents to bare necessity. And you need not worry too much about what to let go of, because the process itself causes much to spontaneously fall away. It is more a process of internal rather than external clearing: it brings to the surface all of your old conditioning, beliefs, and points of view, so that you can see that they no longer fit what you are. But your external life can also change dramatically, especially in the areas where you were functioning out of alignment with your deeper needs. You are forced to become authentic and true to yourself. If you do not you will feel overwhelmed, divided and unhappy.

Once there is an initial arising of kundalini energy, there is likely to be a prolonged period of experiencing random energies, shaking, blocks in the body, rushes in the body that may be startling or pleasurable, ripples of heat and cold, heightened energies followed by exhaustion, and a variety of other phenomena, which will be described in detail in the following chapter.

My energy awakened following an intense body therapy and breathwork session when, later in the day, I was sitting on the floor in a classroom listening to a lecture. It felt like I was being charged over and over again with an electrode at the base of my spine, and with each charge I would feel higher, more ecstatic. This continued periodically for weeks, so that I would walk down the street and feel waves of energy, of love, of seeing the rightness of all things, and I would lay awake at night vibrating and shaking. I felt drawn to sit in meditation for hours, and sometimes fell away into a non-identifiable space from which I would return full of bliss. Sometimes a single part of my body – half of my face, or an arm - would go into bliss. I was my energy, not my mind, and it made me very happy until circumstances in my family life brought the anxious mind back into domination and I came back down to earth. This awakening occurred when I was 41 years old, and had been meditating seriously for much of the past 15 years.

Bob, a man who had taught transcendental meditation for many years, attended a six-week retreat where he spent 12 hours a day in intense energy practices, and when his kundalini activated it rushed through his body like a train, knocking him into a near-unconscious state for several days. He felt like every nerve in his body was on edge, his mind could not focus, and he would sweat profusely at night. Emotional memories would arise, along with involuntary crying and laughing. He felt his life was ricocheting out of control.

Louise had a high-level professional career, and her energy awakened following an intense affair with a spiritually awakened man. She begin to shake involuntarily during the night and as she sat in business meetings it felt like her head was spinning in circles. The energy so overwhelmed her she quit her job to take time to understand what was happening to her, and didn't try to hold a job again for several years. But she became much more creative, and designed a new home at the time.

Joanna, a Buddhist practitioner, began to experience interior vibration when meditating, which made it difficult to hold the lengthy stillness expected in her Buddhist practice setting. She was quivering and shaking and heat was rising into her chest until it was nearly unbearable. She was alarmed and went to a doctor who treated her as if she had a seizure disorder, putting her on medications, and she slowed down her spiritual practice because of her fear. Years later she began to question the diagnosis and she sought out a spiritual perspective.

Steven, following nine years of intense Zen practice, came home from a retreat with a great sense of despair and failure. Sitting in his room he hit the depths of his longing and his sense of inadequacy. Suddenly a gigantic rush of energy poured through his body and pressed against the top of his head. His heart pounded so fast he thought he would pass out and he knew he was going to die. He said to himself, "If that is what it takes to wake up then so be it." At this, the energy burst through the top of his head and his consciousness expanded into a vast and empty spaciousness.

Jeremy was only 19 when he was in a head-on auto accident, and was thrown from the car to the side of the road. Unconscious, he nonetheless witnessed everything that happened, as if hovering above his body, until he awakened in the hospital hours later. After this he had intense rushes of energy through his body, causing much pain in the areas of his neck and back. His spine was seriously injured. He had flashes when he saw apparent other lives, had floating out-of-body experiences, and suffered with strong internal vibrations. Sometimes he saw images of Indian gods and goddesses in his room, although he did not know their origin or meaning. He lost the use of his legs, and all interest in his college studies and friends. Previously an agnostic, he began a deep search to understand the spiritual meaning of his experiences.

These are just a few of the hundreds of ways kundalini may first be known unexpectedly, and initiate a variety of challenges. Here are a few more descriptions taken directly from people in my files:

> I was meditating after doing yoga breathing practices one night and suddenly I felt a burst of energy around my spine. I can only describe it as hot and cold at the same time. It swirled up my spine to the top of my head and then it felt like light was pouring out the top of my head. This lasted a few minutes and then ended. The next day I felt some fluid flowing from the roof of my mouth. It was sweet and had an odd smell. For weeks after I felt flows of energy and this dripping sweetness nearly every day.

***

> I felt a horrible burning pain that shot up my spine and my kidneys felt like they were on fire. My heart hurt and was beating way too fast and I went to a hospital for help, but while talking to the intake person, I realized they couldn't help, so I left. For a few days I had extreme fatigue, could not eat or go

anywhere, and then it flipped into feeling waves of bliss and I felt in love with everyone and everything. I had many spontaneous orgasms, even while driving. For months I went through cycles of bliss and pain, racing pulses, waking in the night doing yoga postures. Sometimes I felt expanded into a golden ball of light.

***

For weeks my feet trembled when I was in bed. Then my lover broke up with me, and for days I felt out of control with weeping and very depressed. My mind began racing, and it felt like energy and a lot of heat was stuck in my head. My body started jerking hard whenever I lay down and I felt emotionally drained for days. The jerking started in the lower chakras and shot into the heart. My head buzzed constantly. For weeks I could not sleep and I would feel terror throughout the night.

***

I was alone in a retreat house and my body felt completely collapsed, but with a huge increase in the internal energy. I felt completely centered in the now, and for several days there was a huge rushing river of powerful energy

running from my feet through my
crown, all day and night. I entered a
vast ocean of infinite blissful energy for
hours, bobbing up and down,
groundless. Every movement I made felt
as if I was moving through an ocean
and as if I had forgotten how to stand,
walk, sit or move. Finally I contacted
my old yoga teacher who helped me get
more in balance and learn a new way to
be in my body.

Kundalini may initially arise partially and
retreat after a single experience, or arise to a specific
chakra area where it seems stuck for months, or
arise through each chakra over a period from days to
years, or shoot suddenly throughout the entire body.
Awakenings may be temporary, incomplete or (very
rarely) complete, depending on the person's lifestyle,
history and practice.

Triggers For Awakening

Kundalini awakening appears to happen in
conjunction with extreme concentration, and during
moments when consciousness shifts away from its
accustomed parameters of identification. This is why
so many spiritual practices encourage one-pointed
concentration, either of the mind, the breath,
through repetitive movement like spinning, or even
by holding the position of the body. Meditation,
prayer, yoga, martial arts, stillness, presence,
intense love, intense focus, the shock of a great
beautiful moment, the shock of a horrific or violent
moment, great despair, great devotion and other

practices and events can shift awareness into the kind of concentration, or what I would term *pure presence*, that is receptive to kundalini arising.

Many people who have awakenings have done one or a variety of spiritual practices for years, and yet many more who do these practices never have an awakening. So there is an additional element, often called grace, that is indefinable, but apparently part of the cause. Whether this grace arises from an external source or an internal shift is hard to say.

Most of the people I have interviewed in this process reported having a longing and an openness to know what is true, to know God, or to understand what life is all about, as a dominant aspect of their life journey since childhood or young adulthood. They come from all religious backgrounds, or none at all, and have felt little ability to find answers to their most pressing concerns through their religious or cultural upbringing. Some were raised in families with spiritual orientations, some in spiritually indifferent families; some came from healthy and loving backgrounds, and others have abusive or destructive family histories. It doesn't seem to matter in terms of one's facility for awakening. Individuals of all ages, either sex, all lifestyles, all countries and all personality styles have had awakenings. People with years of spiritual training, or none at all, have spontaneous awakenings. As awakened spiritual teacher, Adyashanti, likes to tell his students, "God can do this any way it wants."

The major ways that I have seen kundalini awaken, sometimes with positive and sometimes with very difficult reactions include:

- As a response to deep commitment and intensity in meditation, or to great devotional love and prayer.

- After a direct experience of Self-realization which, in this case, precedes the awakening of kundalini, rather than following it.

- After doing energy work such as QiGong, kundalini yoga, Reiki, tantric practices, or therapeutic breathwork.

- Following the step-be-step guidance of an awakened teacher, or receiving a transmission of energy from him or her.

- Enduring a profound emotional event such as overwhelming love, grief or despair, or following traumatic event.

- In response to a powerful place that is approached with great openness, such as pyramids, volcanoes or sacred caves.

- In response to concentrated esoteric practices used to activate psychic abilities or other paranormal experiences.

There is evidence that some ancient dance practices, including Hawaiian Huna, Native American rituals, African rituals, and Egyptian dances that follow the positions of certain temple carvings, may activate kundalini energy. Sexual tantric practices can also activate kundalini, and also sexual engagement with an awakened person.

In the following situations kundalini energy may arise, but is much more likely to be problematic, bringing confusion and more overwhelm into the system, because it happens out of context, so that the person may not be prepared adequately, or has a body that is especially vulnerable. It is not common for kundalini to arise in these situations, but it may occur:

- Enduring a major trauma such as an accident, rape or a mugging.

- A reaction to homeopathy treatments, childbirth or other medical interventions.

- Under the influence of LSD, Ecstasy, marijuana or other mind-altering substances.

- In a sexual relationship with a person who has active kundalini energy.

The Role of Kundalini in Mystical Experience

Many people associate spiritual awakening with mystical experiences. Mystical events include experiences of great light, visions of deities or sacred spaces, a sense of seeing beyond the world of form and into the energy and light that creates them, a sense of being infused with the love of God or the divine, or a sense of hearing sacred music or words

from God or other beings. The awakening of
kundalini energy may happen in conjunction with
these events, and even during dreams related to
these kinds of non-ordinary experiences. However
many people have access to mystical experiences
without the activation of kundalini. This is probably
due to the stimulation of specific areas of the heart
or brain, or a genetic tendency that makes them
more open to altered states of consciousness.

When kundalini activation occurs before or
during a mystical experience it appears that it has
energized certain areas of the subtle body or brain,
which then release imagery, lights, sounds and other
phenomena in some people. (Not everyone
experiences this.) A few people seem able to leave the
body and experience other dimensions. This can be
accompanied by intense bliss, love, or happiness.
These events can seem to fulfill all the person's
longing to know there is indeed another world that is
more beautiful and satisfying than the ordinary
material world in which he or she lives. In some way
these moments build faith in the expansive potential
of consciousness, demonstrating a much broader
range of possibilities, breaking down limitations of
thought and conventionality.

When these experiences happen, the tendency
is to believe they were the goal, and then to attempt
to recreate or hold on to them. Many spiritual
seekers have felt like failures when such events do
not continually recur, or mistakenly believe the goal
is to be in a permanent state of mystical ecstasy and
drama. But in fact these events are a by-product of

the kundalini activation as it moves through and opens up the body and mind, and no one has the capacity to live in them permanently, or produce them deliberately or consistently. Their tendency is to pass away, just as all other phenomena pass away. They may seem to be great gifts, or cause a great disappointment when they fade, but in the final stages of awakening, even these attachments must fall away, or a spiritual seeker can end up in a state of addiction to high experiences, and feel distress about their absence for the rest of his or her life, instead of becoming free. While these are some of the most enjoyable phenomena in this process, like all phenomena they pass, leaving one with simple presence, being the one who witnessed the phenomena. True freedom is moving beyond all clinging and attachments, whether mystical or mundane. It is not a moving beyond enjoyment of either, just releasing the tendency to make demands or have expectations regarding one's experience.

An example of this is an experience I had while meditating one night when I felt compelled to fall on the floor and drifted out of my body into an absorption into light and space that could only be described as seeming as if I were part of the Milky Way. I was lost in this for several hours, as if the mind had melted into the flowing light, until the cold in the room suddenly woke up my body, but the phenomena left me in bliss for hours more.

A friend of mine fell into a quasi-dream state during a difficult time and a guru filled with light and love appeared who gave her specific advice on what she needed to do. This recurred for several weeks as she began to heal, and he gave her specific advice on how she should eat and told her to write a journal about her past history. A few months later she was better, and she saw a magazine with his picture and knew she needed to go to India to become his student.

Here is a man's description of an out-of body experience with mystical features and/or a vision evidently triggered by an encounter with a guru.

> One day as my guru was walking past me I asked him to initiate me into the Gayatri mantra and he said, "Already done." A few days later I found myself safely tucked away in my bed at home chanting the Gayatri mantra till I started to nod off. The next thing I know I am consciously leaving my body and floating upward above my bed, the house, the city, the earth, ever upward until I was flying freely through the universe in my perfected form (mind you, this is not a dream, I am fully aware that I am out of my body). When I say perfected form, it was the form I have now, only perfect in every way, dazzling with brilliant light and energizing sparks (I can remember it as if it were yesterday). After some time I started falling back to earth very, very quickly. I fell into a deep pit on the earth's surface and kept descending until I hit a huge sleeping serpent or

dragon of some kind. I was frightened
as I intuitively felt this creature was
very, very powerful. The serpent chased
me up and out of the abyss and let out a
mighty roar (I can't explain it in words).
Next thing I knew, I found myself back
in bed with a racing heart and sweaty
body. I continued to chant the Gayatri
till the sandman took me over.

There are many descriptions of non-ordinary
or mystical experience in the literature and spiritual
biographies of every tradition. Christian saints have
said they feel they were being made love to by the
Divine. Yogis describe meetings with Gods,
Goddesses and masters on other planes of existence.
These moments can be wonderful to know but can
also be deceptive if we come to believe they are the
answer to self-realization and freedom. For some
people they offer guidance and encouragement in
their practice and direction, strengthening their trust
in something greater than themselves. For others
they include insight, open the heart or offer a new
perception of human experience, or appear to reveal
deeper conflicts and potentials of the psyche through
image and sensation.

The following chapters provide more specific
and comprehensive descriptions of phenomena that
may occur following a kundalini awakening, and will
explore the factors that help this awakening process
move toward spiritual completion.

Chapter 2: Kundalini Phenomena

There are two basic starting points in the kundalini process, the first being a path that is chosen, because a person has a great yearning to find the truth, or has fallen into a practice that will lead them in that direction. The second path is an accident, triggered by some encounter or event in which the awakening occurred unexpectedly. The response to entering the kundalini process is often fear and resistance. It is like becoming disoriented in the woods, and having no idea which direction to take. Occasionally an awakening occurs for no obvious reason at all, a startling encounter with energy in the middle of the night, or during a walk across the lawn. In all of these circumstances, other more disarming events are likely to follow.

Here is a description of a phase in the process sent by a client in her 30's who had trained in Thailand to do healing work, and had many years of spiritual practice. She describes many of the phenomena that may arise suddenly in someone with activated kundalini, including energy, undiagnosed pain, vastness, heightened senses, visions, fear of dying and bliss.

A current of energy, previously unknown to me began to infiltrate the body. A lot of pain in the bones of my pelvis, lovely blissful sensations up my spine. Tons of energy, like I could light up a small city. I began ecstatically dancing every day. I heard bells and music. I could hear conversations three aisles away in the grocery store. I smelled roses and jasmine and citrus. Objects appeared as either completely thin and barely there or as crystal or diamonds. Also during this time, the image of Shakti began to appear during physical love-making. A loss of identity with my personality would occur and spontaneous chanting, or the body would begin moving into mudras and postures. None of this was usual to my experience. Also, Kali began to appear in visions, during love-making. Not really visions. Hallucinations? I don't know. Very real experience with Kali biting my head off or tearing my limbs, saying to me "you are mine". I previously knew nothing of Kali or any of this. I had been a vegetarian for 30 years and now began eating a lot of red meat because Kali required it. And my nervous system would shut down if I didn't eat meat. Life appeared as a miracle of Creation and I felt that my consciousness was existing at the juncture between Creation and matter. It was a time of Fire. And in fact I did have one episode where I felt that I was facing immediate physical death. My bones were being reduced to ash, and I felt as if I was being cremated and would probably not survive. There were several other moments of harrowing physical experiences. I also had a strong feeling that I was losing my mind and would probably end up crazy. I kept telling my husband and close spiritual companions that I was not going to be fit for public life. I could be in yoga class and fall to the floor in a fit of ecstasy and babble just from going into warrior pose.

A few months later I went to bed with what I believed at the time was a toothache in my lower left molar. As the day progressed the amperage running through the left side of my head became severely intense. I still believed I had a toothache, so I made a dentist appointment. Long story short, I spent a month in literal hell with terrible undiagnosed pain in the left side of my head. I tried narcotics and alcohol and marijuana and B vitamins and heat and ice and valerian and arnica and ...and.....and...I was like a wolf in a trap. It did not feel bearable to me. My consciousness shrunk down to nothing but the perception of agonizing physical pain. After about a month of agony, I slowly began to try and crawl my way out of the pain. Acupuncture afforded some relief, and I began doing some research of my own. I found a cranial-sacral healer that I thought might be able to help. During our first session, we were able to calm my nervous system down to what he called a "still point" and it felt like bliss. My mind stopped and I could rest in peace. At this session he told me that I was experiencing kundalini and suggested a few web sites for me to explore.

Seven Categories of Phenomena

In my research with over two thousand people who have had the initiating event of kundalini awakening, I have found seven categories of phenomena that might subsequently occur. I have identified them as pranic activity, involuntary yogic activity, physiological problems, psychological or emotional upheavals, extrasensory experiences, parapsychological experiences and samadhi or satori experiences. Usually everyone does not experience all of these phenomena, but most will experience several of them over a period of months or years.

Pranic Activity or Kriyas

Kriyas are involuntary body movements, shaking, vibrations, jerking, and the sensation of electricity, tingling, or rushes of energy flooding the body. *Kriya* is a Sanscrit word meaning action, and many *kriyas* mimic the postures taught in hatha yoga called *asanas*, or hand gestures called *mudras*.

Sometimes people wake up in the middle of the night and their body spontaneously moves into a yoga posture, or performs a gesture with their hands that is used in yoga to bring peace or focus. Most often it is the shaking, internal quivering, or jerks of the body that cause people alarm. These movements are unfamiliar, and so they are interpreted as a sign of illness, even though their true function is simply a restructuring of the subtle field that may ultimately strengthen the flexibility of the body.

Sometimes *kriyas* are gentle, even blissful, and at other times they feel sharp and very uncomfortable. Generally they are not painful, even though the body may appear to be writhing or having a spasm. Sometimes they seem concentrated on an area where there is a contraction or blockage, for example in the belly with someone who has power and control issues, or at the throat when true expression has been repressed for many years, or a person is afraid to say what he or she believes. They may seem to be working in areas where there is a physical weakness as if to rewire it, or to be releasing the stress of emotion or tension carried through the body after a hard days work, or a particularly emotional event. Their function is release, not only of the day's stressors, but those of this life, and possibly genetic or previous life patterns held in the subtle energy body.

Sometimes people experience *kriyas* who have not had an awakening of kundalini, but instead the cells are releasing some contracted energy or life experience, usually following a therapy or bodywork or yoga session, or during an intense emotional or sexual experience. They are one way a body can release stress or blockages.

Other Involuntary Energy Phenomena

In addition to the *kriya* activity that looks like yogic postures or hand movements, symbolic images or geometric patterns may appear during a kundalini process. Sometimes the mind produces a series of images of other worlds, or scenes that cannot be related to the current life. There may also arise the sound of chanting, Sanscrit words and tones, or a variety of specific sounds such as bees buzzing, or kettle drums beating. One client of mine heard many Sanscrit chants and had no idea what they were, or what language it was, until a friend invited her to an Indian *kirtan*, which is the singing of sacred music and chants, and she recognized the songs.

Some people spontaneously create and enter into a ritual. They may think of this as spiritual or just symbolic of something moving inside of them. One woman I interviewed felt compelled to bathe in salt-water, and would dump boxes of it into the bathtub. Another person felt compelled to sort out all the silverware and other kitchen objects into male and female categories. Some people feel a need to purify their home, thoroughly cleaning everything. One woman moved into an Indian tepee on her property and lived in it for nearly a year. Others go on a pilgrimage. While there is a part of the mind that is watching, feeling alarmed by these impulses, and able to stop if the situation requires it, there is a felt sense of urgency, as if an inner dictate wants to work something out on a physical level. Such activity usually occurs only once or twice and does not become compulsive.

Physiological Problems

Kundalini works mysteriously with physical issues, sometimes curing an illness, and at other times bringing something that is latent to the surface. One man wrote to me that kundalini had mysteriously cured him of diabetes. Another reported he no longer had a heart irregularity that had shown up on two previous EKG's.

In addition to the tendency of kundalini to find problems, the stress of the highly amplified energy can cause physical problems such as adrenal exhaustion, hormonal imbalances, short-term visual dysfunction, headaches, burning sensations, back pain and other discomforts. Sometimes problems arise that are pseudo-illnesses: that is, they cannot be explained medically, and defy any diagnosis, and change their nature unexpectedly, moving from one part of the body to another. There can be apparent heart problems, gastrointestinal disorders, nervous energy and hyper-activity, eating disorders, dramatic rushes of heat and cold, pains occurring in back, head, stomach, or big toes. These and other unusual difficulties are atypical and often prove difficult to diagnose and treat because they are not consistent with known illness, and they come and go randomly.

One issue that arises for some people is an over-stimulation of their energy field, leading to hormonal difficulties, adrenal exhaustion, thyroid issues and other factors. They jump out of hyper-activity into profound exhaustion and energy depletion. It is as if they have blown up their chemical and nervous systems. Usually this is the result of too frequent or intense energy practices. All practices that manipulate energy and consciousness can become overwhelming if done too frequently. Some people do Tantra practices, Qigong, and energy healing all in a day. Or they may do shamanic practices, heavy fasting, breathwork and kundalini yoga in a 2-week period. Bodies can only handle a certain level of energy arousal at a time. A person in this process needs to listen to their deepest intuition about what the system needs and pull back from too much activity, balancing it with quiet and grounding time in their lives.

When there are conditions that appear to be serious, such as chest or stomach pain, or headaches, it is advisable to have a medical evaluation. It is possible to have a serious illness along with a kundalini arising, not caused by the latter but concurrent with it. If there are genuine symptoms of disease, then it is important to get treatment, because no degree of spiritual attainment can prevent you from getting a life threatening illness. (Every famous guru has ultimately released their physical body, several because of diabetes or cancer.) On the other hand, if there is no medical explanation for the problem, and if the symptoms do not occur with any consistency, then it is a relief to attribute them to the spiritual process.

It is not uncommon to experience great shifts in eating and sexual patterns after kundalini arises. Many people feel compelled to give up certain foods, drugs and alcohol, and some lose interest in food or sex for brief periods of time, or even longer. It is important to eat a modest amount of healthy food during this time, to keep up your strength and energy, and avoid becoming "spacy" or nervous. Eating root vegetables, protein drinks, a bit of brown rice or heavy bread can all be helpful. I strongly recommend that people in this process have a consultation with an Ayurvedic practitioner who can suggest the best foods and herbal supplements for a person's particular energy system in the condition it may be in at this time. Ayurveda, the medicine of India, identifies specific diets for various body-types, remedies for imbalances in each type of system, and a complete system for harmonizing subtle body energies for health and well-being.

One of the most commonly reported issues after kundalini arises is insomnia. This is an ancient and well-documented problem. In tantric literature it is suggested that one simply recognize that they need much less sleep and do something useful with the time, like meditation or spiritual reading. If someone meditates a great deal of time his or her actual need for sleep is diminished. Also the energies tend to run more actively at night when we are in a more sedentary state. Once you realize you do not need as much sleep as in the past it is helpful to let go of thoughts and worries about it and find a way to enjoy the extra time. However if you have many nights with very little sleep you may need to take a day to nap, or use a mild sleep assistant such as melatonin to assure you do not become disoriented. Some people become irrational or mentally hazy when sleep deprived, and behavior can even appear psychotic. Listen to your body and catch up with sleep if you feel physically or mentally exhausted. You can drink warm milk, take time for daily exercise, listen to sleep inducing tapes, and invite peaceful imaging to encourage the body to let go and rest. Sometimes counting your breaths backwards from one hundred can be helpful. One teacher told me he looks for some part of his body that is ready to sleep and then puts his attention there.

Psychological and Emotional Upheavals

Sometimes awakening is accompanied by an intensification of unresolved psychological issues, fear of death or insanity, mood swings, or crushing waves of anxiety, anger, guilt, or depression, and this surge of feeling may seem to be unrelated to any personal issues. One may also experience waves of compassion, unconditional love, and heightened sensitivity to the moods of others. People are particularly prone to fall in love with inappropriate love objects during this time: that is, someone unattainable, or of an age and sex that would not have attracted them in the past. Love may arise and suddenly fall without discrimination upon everyone.

Remember that this is a clearing process, and all the energies woven into your subtle field and related to your life experiences are unraveling. This brings an opportunity to look at and release all that has been hidden or held secretly as the foundation of your beliefs about your life. Subtle energies hold the patterns of your emotional responses, and hold together a "memory" of who you are that you wake up to every morning. Sometimes it seems that the emotions of this life, previous lives, and even collective lives, are expressing through your body, and you have no idea why, nor any memory you can call up to explain it.

Through all this upheaval, if you can manage to develop self-compassion and silent witnessing, it will serve you well when you reach a stage of embodiment in your spiritual process. In order to hold the vast love and wisdom that we essentially are, we must clear out our impressions of ourselves and others, let go of emotional stances and self-destructive ideas, and become free of our history. In a nutshell, this is why we go through upheaval in this process. Deconstruction of the identity is an inevitable correlation of a complete spiritual awakening, and is discussed in more depth in the second volume of this set, "The Awakening Guide".

Extrasensory Experiences

It appears that extra senses can activate when kundalini awakens, and some ancient scriptures say it is possible for the vision and hearing to become much more acute, even becoming super-human: for example, one might see the ants crawling up a tree in the distance, or hear whispers from another room. More commonly, people may experience unfamiliar and spontaneous visual images, such as of lights, symbols, and entities, or the reviewing of other lives, or visions that are felt to be psychologically or spiritually meaningful.

A few times I have heard descriptions by people who have experienced a radical change of environment, where the surroundings shift for a moment into another historical time, become black and white, or appear to be in some other place. One woman, driving over a bridge, suddenly lost her bearings and felt she was out in space. Another saw frightful demonic images in the sky outside her 9th floor window. (I believe this was a personification of some extreme anger and despair she was experiencing). Some people may occasionally hear sounds, a voice, music or a helpful phrase from scripture. They may smell sandalwood, perfume or incense, or some other fragrance of their childhood i.e. cooking, although they know it is not present in the room. These kinds of events can be very disarming, especially as they are associated in most people's minds with mental illness or psychosis. When the situation is triggered by kundalini, these events are very occasional, rarely threatening, and soon pass away. When they have elements of danger (such as the demonic images) they suggest an underlying psychological issue, or the residual of working with occult arts, that will probably need to be addressed in therapy.

Parapsychological Experiences

Psychic awareness, unusual synchronicities, healing abilities, seeing or feeling auras, channeling, electrical sensitivity, remote viewing (seeing an event happening somewhere else) and psycho-kinesis (objects moving without being touched) are the most commonly reported parapsychological phenomena. Sometimes there is dramatically awakened creativity, far beyond what the person ever accomplished before. Amazing art and music have emerged in this process. While there is nothing wrong with having any of these experiences, becoming attached to acquiring these kinds of gifts can lead to spiritual cul-de-sacs, where one may be distracted from realization for a lifetime.

Many people find as consciousness becomes more full or alive in them their psychic capacity changes, and they may have an interior message when a family member is ill or dying, a flash about an impending event, or simply be thinking of a distant friend before they suddenly call. For example, one woman felt compelled to turn around and drive to her father's home one day, and on arriving discovered he had just suffered a stroke. Of course many people are psychically sensitive who are not in a spiritual process, and in the teachings of kundalini science, this is thought to be related to brain centers that are more open in some people than in others.

I have known people who felt they lived in a magical world for a while, with everything happening exactly as they needed it to, and synchronicities (something like a fortuitous coincidence) led their lives. Suddenly this ended, and they feared they had lost their awakening. But these kinds of events are not awakening at all, only ways that consciousness seems to support the movement while a person is in certain stages of the journey. All of us experience synchronicity at times, but often we do not notice, or we label it coincidence and let it pass. These events are much more common in a kundalini process.

Some people find themselves spontaneously performing healing after a kundalini arising, moving to help a person or an animal who is hurt, and finding they make a huge difference. One woman I worked with, who had never known anything about healing, felt compelled to stop at the scene of an accident and stop the bleeding of an injured passenger. Later she found energy flowing out of her hands, and an inner guide that would tell her what a person needed and move her hands involuntarily to areas that needed help. Her process clearly was similar to the way the QiGong energy healers work, although she did not know this. She has continued her focus on spiritual awakening, but allowed this healing work to develop, taking no income from it but doing it as a service that feels aligned with her deepest Self. From the place of healing she is not a separate individual, but stands in the emptiness or presence of the vastness she knows herself to be. Because she is not identified with it, this work will probably not become a cul-de-sac for her, but if she were to become identified and create a personal conceptual or professional framework around it, this could slow down her capacity for self-realization. It could become a new identity to be melted away before she would be free.

Another client came to me because her kundalini process was causing her to pass out, and after seeing a program on TV related to UFO's she felt she might have been abducted. When she went into a hypnotic state the story that came forward was not about modern aliens, but about ancient Egypt, and she began to channel an entity that appeared to be a light being that had merged with her in a ritual in the pyramids in a previous life. After this we had several sessions in which she channeled this being of light, and in time it became an inner ally for her. This process slowly brought about an integration of her energies and her spiritual expression in the world, moving her to study various spiritual systems, ending her phases of passing out, quieting her energy, moving her through both psychic and healing phases, until the intensity relaxed and she returned into an ordinary life as a grandmother, artist and rancher.

Electrical sensitivity is a topic well researched by the notable near-death researcher, Dr. Kenneth Ring, who found that many people who had near-death experiences reported an odd relationship with electrical objects, being unable to wear watches because they would stop working, having a tendency to short-out appliances and computers, and even making streetlights blink or go out as they walked beneath them. A small percentage of people find this happening during stages of kundalini awakening, as if their whole subtle energy field simply overwhelms the field of relative energy around them.

Psychokinesis is a similar phenomenon, in which objects tend to move spontaneously across a table or fall off a mantel, in the presence of someone with a high pranic energy field. Some systems of energy-manipulation teach methods of using mental concentration to accomplish this directly. I have also participated in what is called a Psi-party, in which a group of several hundred people were taught how to bend metal objects, such as spoons, by concentrated thought, and most people were able to do this within an hour in that environment. The children present were particularly adept at this because they had no preconceived notions that it couldn't be done. I have witnessed similar practices used to make seeds sprout within minutes, and to bend metal bars. This is not spiritual awakening, but rather playing energy games, and it does not require kundalini arousal to accomplish it. However it demonstrates the potential of the underused human psyche.

Samadhi or Satori Experiences

For the purposes of this book I will define samadhi experiences as absorption of consciousness into mystical states of unity, peace, light or energy, sometimes with a clear perception of existential truths, even Self-realization. (There are many levels of samadhi in Sanscrit scriptures). Satori is defined as a glimpse of Truth, a profound sense of, "I am not existent as a separate being yet I am everything" or, "This pure and open consciousness with no identity is what I truly am". It is an experience that cannot be described as it is beyond thought, but it is intuitively known, almost a cellular realization. There may be less intense trance-like states that bring peace, joy, or waves of bliss. A Christian falling into ecstasy or divine union that is free of thought or self-reflection would be the equivalent of one level of samadhi experience. These may occur during or after meditation, or spontaneously at other times.

Please note that any of these phenomena can occur independent of a kundalini awakening, for various reasons. But if a person has had a dramatic initiating event, and this is followed over time with experiences from several of these categories they are probably in a kundalini process.

Why Phenomena Happens

Although we must acknowledge a great mystery in this process of deconstruction that accompanies spiritual awakening, it appears that the primary reason these phenomena arise is that the subtle body field needs to reorganize and become more open. When the subtle body (the field of mind, emotions and senses) is influenced by the quickening energies of kundalini, it releases blocked trauma and pain, along with repressed memories and emotions, and opens the energy field into new experiences which have not been known before, including the opening of brain centers with capacities that are not commonly utilized in ordinary mental states. This is consistent with the teachings of kundalini science, as understood by practitioners in India.

All of our conditioning, which has shaped our patterns of thinking and perceiving what is happening to us, is woven into the subtle energy body field. When kundalini arises, either before or after a spiritual realization, this conditioning is coming undone. Our structure of identification, how we think of who we are, is falling apart. For some unfortunate people, the outside world, and all the crutches of personal identity, will also fall apart. I have heard a few dramatic stories of spiritual initiations that were followed by exterior losses of jobs, homes, lovers, and friends dropping away, in conjunction with the inward collapse of personal identity during this process. This is one form of the dark night of the soul consistently referred to in spiritual literature. This is not a random destruction, however, but instead it is a stripping away of anything that is not truly authentic. The person is being invited to live in a new way.

Gradual and Direct Paths

Having been involved deeply in Ashtanga yoga, kundalini yoga, Advaita Vedanta, and Zen Buddhist traditions, I have seen two interesting patterns that occur in those who have full awakenings to their true nature. Those who teach the gradual path to awakening, such as the eight-limbed yoga of Patanjali, the Kriya Yoga path introduced by Swami Paramahansa Yogananda, or kundalini tantra practices, believe that one must be fully prepared. They offer a process in which yoga and meditation practices awaken the latent coiled energy of kundalini, then move it through correct channels up the spine until it reaches the crown, where a person may experience the bliss and fullness of *samadhi* or *satori* states that reveal the nature of Self. Many Buddhist paths and Sufi paths also follow a gradual training program, leading to the awakening of consciousness, without an emphasis on kundalini arising (although it usually does anyway).

Along the *gradual path* many chaotic events may occur, along with psychological traumas and revelations, and spiritual experiences. There can be many openings of heart and mind, insights, and other positive events, so there is a sense of moving forward to a particular completion, especially if a teacher is at hand who knows the territory. A qualified teacher can tell from the reported experience just where the kundalini energy or spiritual process is activated or blocked.

On the *direct path*, for example in Advaita Vedanta or Zen Buddhism, realization of Truth may occur first, before signs of kundalini energy arise. Traditional Advaita Vedanta teaches that understanding the scriptural teachings is essential, but more modern teachers focus on sudden insight through transmission. Insight may happen while reading a scripture, hearing the Truth clearly spoken, or being in the presence of a teacher who lives it. (Practically speaking, years of long silent meditation periods are also part of the Zen path.) There is a sudden recognition that might be called "I am that!" -- a movement of the psyche that cannot adequately be described, but shifts identity outside of its narrow boundaries and into a vast emptiness, spaciousness and timelessness that shatters any illusion of a separate self. This is awakening. As the Buddha reported simply, "I am awake".

Those who have such awakenings suddenly, when they have never been on a gradual spiritual path, will probably find later that the deconstruction associated with kundalini moves in to support their realization.

Thomas Keating, a Catholic monk, who wrote several books about a meditation process called Centering Prayer that is part of Christian contemplation, calls this deconstruction an unloading of the unconscious. Other systems have called it purification, or clearing. If a person feels either inflated or dejected by this challenging drama of psychological release, and has no understanding of its function, he or she can stay stuck in this cul-de-sac of suffering for a long time.

Along with the turmoil of having all the unfinished psychological issues arise, people may remember apparent other lives, open up psychic and healing potentials, and feel extremely different inside, as if unfamiliar with how to live their lives, since they now feel unable to follow prior interests and drives. They may fall into unpredictable emotional states. This can lead to another form of the dark night of the soul: the sense "I had it, and now I've lost it." There is a great distress that something has gone wrong, because after such a mind-altering realization they believe they should be healed of everything that ever bothered them, and are horrified to find themselves caught again in an old and painful memory or habit. But in time the personal system surrenders, and the past drops away. There is a new openness, followed by more clarity in perceiving the underlying nature of their being, and with this, contentment and peace.

Fortunately, there are many paths to kundalini awakening and to spiritual realization, because there are many personality styles and tendencies on the planet, and nature has provided a great range of opportunities to thrust us inward in order to recognize the truth of our being.

Gradual paths have the advantage of providing understanding (although this may be limited by the style of teaching), training, discipline, community support and modeling, if led by competent and awakened teachers. Ideally, the body and mind become more open and flexible along the way, and the lifestyle becomes more simple and positive. They have a disadvantage in that many people follow them for 20 or 30 years without awakening, and may feel they are "going somewhere," without ever knowing a sense of completion.

Direct paths can be taught through direct clarity, or with obtuse phrases aimed at knocking down logical patterns of thought, such as with the mind-bending *koans* used in certain schools of Zen. The goal is to wake up, to shift consciousness radically, without concern about the impact on the body and psyche. It appears that those who awaken on a direct path are able to transform their lives in accordance with the Truth only to the extent they were *ready* to hear the Truth. This is an approach that is powerful for those who are ready, but may be either distressing or irrelevant to those who are not.

In the end, either path can lead to awakening or disappointment, and the outcome lies in the receptivity of the student, the depth of awakened spirit in the teacher, and a third element that can only be called grace.

Kundalini in Children

Occasionally it happens that a partial or temporary awakening of kundalini happens in childhood. It is also recognized in tantric traditions that people can be born with kundalini energy partially or fully awakened. In a partial arising they may appear to be unusual children with psychic insights, unusual gifts, or wisdom beyond their years. They may have tendencies toward either day-dreaming or hyper-activity. Those few who have entered life with fully awakened kundalini may become remarkably brilliant or wise leaders, creators, poets or innovators in the world.

If a person has come into life with a partial awakening they may at some point begin to experience many or most of the phenomena of awakening, only without the initiating event that characterizes it for others. They may also be greatly misunderstood in a society that values conformity in its children. When they are drawn toward a spiritual practice they may exhibit rapid awakening and evolution, beyond what their teacher would expect.

Many people have reported to me non-ordinary events in childhood, such as a sense of flying, a visitor sitting at the end of their bed with advice, a prediction of a coming event, a ghost or spirit appearing in the room, or a sense of love protecting them during difficult times. One woman reported having a tea party with Mother Mary during the times she was being sexually abused. Usually these experiences are not accompanied by a rising of energy, or if so, the adult did not remember it, and they fade away in adulthood, so they are not likely to be kundalini-related, but rather appear as brief paranormal or mystical openings. Here is a man's childhood story, however, that included an intense energy rising, unfortunately framed in the context of a family that was unpredictable, violent, and sexually abusive. I believe it is possible that sexual abuse occasionally causes a premature awakening of kundalini energy in a child who is not otherwise matured enough physiologically before puberty to sustain a kundalini arising.

> When I was about 8 years old my family life was quite traumatic, and my house was like a battleground most of time. One night, after being screamed at by my mother, I prayed to God. "If you are really out there, can you help me out?" Then for a few weeks a lot of odd things started happening. Lying in my bed I felt as if I was being stretched from the inside out. I'd leave my body at night and look down at myself sleeping. I could travel through my house along the ceiling, and then out into the street and down the road. I also couldn't keep down food, and was crying a lot.

> But the main thing I remember was the feeling of being stretched. I saw an analogy later on a kundalini website that described it perfectly. It was "like the water pressure from a fire hose going through a garden hose." At some point it became extremely hot, and excruciatingly painful. I remember being overwhelmed by the pain. It felt as if something very "thick" or very "solid" was coming up into me from the soles of

my feet and up into my body. Every night it would work its way up to a point, first to my ankles and then my knees, and then lessen in intensity and go back down. The next night it would return and do the same thing, this time going up a bit further into my body. It was always incredibly painful.

One night though, it kept coming up. It went up into my head, and then in a rush, I felt like I was shooting out of my body on it. I felt incredibly happy and remember saying, "I remember, I remember." It's a long time ago but I do remember this very clearly. For a few days after I felt as if I was in a huge space, and remember seeing the vivid glowing colors of flowers like they were actually lights, like they were casting off a haze of bright color. I had a bursting feeling of happiness for short periods of time and saw everything shining, or as if it was an enormous space with me.

How all this ended is very clear in my mind. I was very sexual for a young kid – and around this time I had some kind of sexual experience with another kid. Afterwards, when I was coming home, I distinctly remember a sudden jolt in my center. All the lightness and emptiness inside me disappeared, and I felt full of despair.

It is possible that some of these descriptions are related to repressed sexual abuse, framed in the child's mind in a way that excluded the perpetrator, especially the great pain in the experience. But the aftermath of the energy bursting through the head, and the extended days of beauty and happiness, supports the likelihood of the kundalini arising.

It is very common to lose the blessing of an awakening when we are distracted and re-identify with our bodies and the limitations or difficulties in our lives. Children would be especially vulnerable to this, having no context or understanding of the experience, and often struggling with other issues too overwhelming to manage. Traumas in early life may set the stage for a lifetime of feeling they do not fit in anywhere, with under-developed ego structures and therefore challenges in work and relationship, but searching deeply to find a true validation for the remembering they have known. This may lead to enlightenment, or to isolation and a sense of loss.

One young man I met in a facility that provided job training for the mentally ill was an expert mapmaker. He had had an experience at 5 years old of falling off a couch and breaking his collarbone. He passed out and during this time felt he had a direct experience with Jesus, while being bathed in golden light and blissful energy. When he later tried to tell his family about this he was told he was talking crazy and not to say these things. Over the years he became labeled as mentally ill, was periodically institutionalized and heavily medicated, and the illness became his identity in the world.

Until recent years any mention of mystical experience was described in the diagnostic manual for psychiatry as evidence of psychosis. But in the early development of psychology, the great innovator Richard Bucke wrote a book called "Cosmic Consciousness", in which he described his own spiritual experience and theorized about others. Several other prominent psychiatrists and psychologists, among them William James, Swiss psychiatrist Carl Jung, and Italian psychiatrist Roberto Assagioli, have explored spiritual experiences in their writings, and in the developing field of transpersonal psychology it is reemerging as a valid aspect of human maturation.

Chapter 3: Chaos and Challenge

Every journey has its unexpected elements, perhaps a tempting detour that brings you to a new place you never would have known about, or a meeting with a charming stranger who gives you new insight about the country and its people, and sometimes a period of panic when you become lost and don't know the language, and have forgotten the name of your hotel. (This happened to me once in a crowd in New Delhi, India.)

Somehow we survive both the excitement and the challenges of our life journeys, and we probably survive the kundalini process drawing on the same resources that saw us through the difficulties on the relative level. We will tend to deal with kundalini in ways similar to how we deal with other situations in our life: investigation, reaction, helplessness, anxiety, argumentativeness, openness, contraction, etc. We may find that our old approaches are not much help, and we have to throw ourselves into many new possibilities as we try to work though this experience.

In this chapter we will look at a few of the
major hurdles described by people who experience
this awakening, and suggest the mental attitudes
and physical strengths that are most supportive for
this process. In the classical method of dealing with
this energy one would spend many years with a
teacher, who would offer guidance such as specific
breathing and meditation practices from one stage to
the next, and require a discipline regarding diet,
lifestyle, sexuality, service, obedience, study and
spiritual practice. In some spiritual systems, like
Tibetan Buddhism, great complex visualizations
enable one to see through the workings of mind in
order to collapse the dependence and beliefs related
to the illusory self, long before awakening occurs.
Other traditions use energy practices, sound
practices, the development of compassion, or a
dedication to karma yoga, which is basically steady
work and service without any attachment to the
results, all of which are long-standing methodologies
for breaking down attachment to the ego, and
preparing or cleansing the mind, in order to facilitate
a fruitful and stable awakening experience.

Given this historic approach to awakening
energy and consciousness into a new life, it is not so
surprising that westerners, who come into the
process with no training or preparation, are
sometimes knocked into heavy physical and
emotional experiences that disturb them. There are
four specific challenges in this process that are
possibly more common in westerners, and are little
discussed in spiritual literature because in classic
times the preparation dissipated the problem before

it arose. These are not experiences common to everyone, but are situations I have often seen in my work. They are:

1) A sudden awakening can feel like a major threat to the physical body.

2) A psychological reaction of depression, rage or anxiety related to changes in energy, interests, and personal identification.

3) A terror of emptiness, or of darkness.

4) Special issues arising due to sexual or physical abuse in childhood.

When the Body Feels Threatened

Lorraine had a dramatic awakening of energy following a weekend workshop with a QiGong master from China, when she was 49. Before this weekend she had been suffering with severe back pain, to the point she spent hours laying in bed. Prior to this she had spent 20 years working as a hospice director, sitting for hours with people who were dying, and her life had been very service oriented in a spiritual way, although she would not have called herself a spiritual seeker. After two days of practicing QiGong, Lorraine's pain left her body and she felt open and energized, and then suddenly huge rushes of energy took her over, along with heat, and a continual elimination of fecal matter and other liquids from her body. She was so hot she felt she was on fire, and she was incapacitated by stomach gurgling, and a need to be near the bathroom. Her body shook and she couldn't eat or sleep. At times she felt paralyzed, curled in a fetal position on the floor. She wondered if she was dying, while at the same some part of her mind was telling her that this was really okay. This process continued for about five days, and then gradually dissipated, leaving her exhausted and confused, but healed from her previous physical problems. She felt different inside, but could not define exactly how. A few months later she was at the scene of an automobile accident and felt compelled to help an injured person by the road. Her touch seemed to calm and heal him, and she discovered an inner directive that advised her what to do to and simply followed. After this she began to explore healing with friends and family, and a Chinese guide seemed to assist her and direct her from another dimension as she opened her consciousness and moved her own personality out of the way. Over the next two years she learned about the kundalini process, and was advised to integrate her life into the process, which she has done with great success.

***

James was a college student, working on his M.S. in economics, when he had a powerful energy awakening while using LSD. His body shook for hours, and he felt as if his mind had shattered and opened into the sky, while his nervous system was shot, and he couldn't sleep for several days. He ended up in a psychiatric ward when his thoughts became convoluted and his expression manic, and he was found walking on the beach at night crying and laughing and talking to an entity. Following a few days of sleep and medication his thinking function became more normal, and he was able to leave the hospital, but he felt fragile, nervous, and unable to focus on his schoolwork, and dropped out of school. A friend took him in and he spent several weeks with her, living a very simple life, afraid he would never be able to function again. In time he began a journey to find a teacher, understanding, and a new life direction, having lost all interest in the college courses he had been pursuing. Over the years he developed a spiritual orientation, returned to college to become a psychotherapist, and had a successful career.

***

Margery was crippled by polio at the age of 14, and lived in a high-rise apartment with her mother. When she was 24 a yogi came to visit her mother and came into her bedroom, offering to give her healing energy. He placed her hands on her and she began to shake, and she felt a great wave of energy move through her body. After he left the energy rushes continued, and she began to see visions of demonic energies outside her window, which was nine stories up from a busy street. This went on for several years, and she tried to contact the yogi, and the center where he had lived, but no one was willing to see her again or offer any advice. She was greatly distressed that there was no improvement in her health, and now there was a serious distortion in her mind.

***

Lisa was pregnant, and had a late term miscarriage. She nearly died in the hospital and was ill for weeks afterwards. She went to a homeopath to regain her strength and was put on an intense formula that apparently triggered a massive reaction of energy rushes and panic, which continued for many months. She was bedridden because of pain in her belly and energy vibrations she could not manage, and she was diagnosed with panic attack disorder. She lived in a community headed by a lama, but no one there had any advice related to her energy process, probably because it had happened out of context from the way it was supposed to in the Tibetan tradition, so it was not interpreted as having anything to do with her spiritual life.

All of these situations, culled from my files, are stories of people who came into an energy awakening with no preparation, no understanding, and no support to help them through it. As a therapist who has specialized in this field I have heard hundreds of variations of these stories.

Sometimes I am asked if kundalini is dangerous, and I usually say it does not need to be, because I believe that fear in the receiver of this energy magnifies the difficulty of the experience. The function of kundalini awakening is positive, being a natural movement of consciousness to clear the way for a peaceful and wise life. But fear is inevitable if you have no context for such an experience, do not see any spiritual or physical advantage to it, and believe that it is destroying your life. And there are significant difficulties when it awakens out of the context of one's understanding, or during a traumatic event. This would rarely happen to a person living in spiritual community under the guidance of a true teacher, although in some cases the community has such a narrow paradigm for its occurrence that students are considered at fault when the energy awakens in a chaotic way. This can be crippling to their spiritual process. In one case, a student of mine had contacted the head of a major community that teaches Kriya Yoga, which is a gradual process for awakening kundalini, and asked for help with his energy problems. Her response to him was, "This can't be kundalini, because kundalini is always positive!"

If an awakening of energy occurs in a way that is sudden and overwhelming, there is not a lot you can do, other than surrender to it. If you bring consciousness deeply into your center and invite the energy to do what it must, in as gentle a way as possible, you may find a place inside, as Lorraine did, that already knows it is okay. This is a part of you that is already awake and clear, and does not see what happens to the body as especially significant. It trusts that this is work that now will be done because it is your time to do it. You may feel it is a mistake, or caused by an encounter you did not invite, but it is clearly your destiny, or karma, or it would not have happened.

It is impossible to answer the question, "Why did this happen to me?" just as you cannot answer it in any given crisis. There is an element of fate, and if we spin our wheels seeking who to blame, we only distract ourselves from the real issues, which are: "Where can this take me?" and "How can I come to terms with it?" The sooner we meet the situation, and accept it with grace and equanimity, the sooner we can find a new place to stand in consciousness, one that includes the wider vision of what it means to be human and alive.

The first step in finding this equanimity is understanding, or discovering a context for this radical downloading of old energies, and this major upswelling of new ones. Whatever has been stored in the cells, in the energy system -- all the suffering, drama, pain or loss or grief -- will be released in this process. It can be felt physically in a very intense way, as in these cases, or gradually leak out over a long period of time, without so much drama. In the case of Lorraine, my sense is that by sitting with death for so many thousands of hours in hospice she had prepared herself for an awakening, but her body needed to release all the holding of suffering she had taken in for others. I have had many clients with a background in hospice care, and believe sitting in such concentrated and transitional moments, makes the psyche more ripe for an awakening, just as meditation does.

In the case of James, I believe the LSD triggered a quantum leap before his body/mind was ready for it, and so he was very vulnerable. It is like going into zero gravity without astronaut training. It's a huge leap for the body/mind and can leave one in extreme states of confusion and exhaustion, overcharging and burning out the nervous system. So when this happens it is essential to take time to recuperate, eat properly, avoid stress, and strengthen or renew the physical body, however long it may take. In addition, yogis believe that drugs cause toxins to remain in the body, which inhibit the correct movement of energy until they have worked their way out of the system.

In the case of Margery, it seems to me she was dealt with irresponsibly by a yogi who had an inflated idea related to his own power. She was opened emotionally and psychically in ways she had no control over, and so her suffering and darker thoughts about her life circumstances were externalized as demonic forces. The mind can create and enter many dimensions, and our emotional states often make us vulnerable to entering a dark and fearful realm. Without a teacher who can help us navigate and integrate these forces we can be stuck for a long time. In these situations one needs therapy to heal the psychic pain and splits, and spiritual guidance to find the light of awake presence in oneself. Knowing our true nature allows us to transcend the limitations of our physical situation.

Lisa was prepared in a way for the awakening because of her Buddhist practice, and eventually brought it into a spiritual context. She had to recognize what was happening and claim her own truth, because a teacher could not, or chose not, to provide understanding for her. The body itself becomes overwhelmed by trauma at times, and this physical overwhelm is like a near-death experience, opening the energy as if one was dying, in which case kundalini would be unraveling to leave the body. Of course she did not die, but the dynamic energy stayed present and did not recoil itself. It took her many years of spiritual study and practice, and finding her way as a writer and teacher to help others in panic situations, to find her own ground of equanimity. Some people find the doorway into wisdom and compassion is full of pain, but once they have passed through they have much to teach others who are caught in suffering.

If you are having a great deal of physiological response to a kundalini awakening, it is advisable to get a medical evaluation. The energy can put great stresses on the heart, adrenal system, nervous system, electrolytes, or hormonal balance. The body can indeed respond with chaos. A good medical workup can help you by identifying anything that needs addressing to become a stronger and healthier vehicle in this process, and relieve the mind from worrying about conditions that are not pathological, but simply part of the energy process.

Psychological Reactions to Change

Once a person has had a glimpse of their true nature, he or she is likely to find chunks of personal identity falling away, like an ice cap that is melting fast. The tendency may be to grasp, to hold on to something that used to have meaning, or offer comfort, and give a sense of belonging. But it doesn't seem to work, this grasping, and instead one may feel fear, grief, or doubts about their sanity, when they notice how their mind is changing. It is natural to feel these things when we are losing parts of ourselves. It is natural to grieve for a little while. But if we make up a story about being someone who has lost so much, we are only creating a new identity, as mind prefers believing in something negative to facing its own insignificance.

Our minds are tools, and like the modern science fiction tale of a computer run amuck and trying to control those who created it, our minds have overestimated their own importance. Thought continually flows through us, as synapses collide, pouring into our field all the associations of our personal experience and many collective ideas and dictates. This has been such a steady stream for so long that we have come to believe this is who we are, this collection of thoughts, memories and identities. It is apparently a system designed to hold individuals in separation so that the One wholeness can play a multitude of roles and live as humanity and creation, and it is useful in terms of our capacity to relate, create and enjoy the forms we are. The working mind has an important role. The bossy overseer part of mind constricts our ability to know our true nature.

The capacity of mind is more limited than the capacity of Self, which is all-inclusive, and its role needs to be relegated to the background, used for practical applications in the relative world. There is actually a natural dropping away of the self-criticism and inner chatter about "my" life, once a deep awakening occurs. The overseer, or what Freud called the super-ego, may have little influence any longer, once it is clear that there is no separate self, and everything that happened in our past was simply a string of events about which we no longer need to concern ourselves.

It is disarming when old desires, belief systems, friendships or jobs lose their meaning and carry no intrinsic satisfaction. It is usually unexpected, because if you thought of yourself as a spiritual person you were probably working hard at all of these things, and no one told you that giving up everything meant literally an internal giving up of everything. But once you relax into this letting go, and begin to feel the freedom of being present wherever you are without demands or expectations, your body/mind begins to experience a kind of contentment you have never known, a happiness independent of anything that could ever be gained or acquired. You find it underneath the rubble of your old conditioned personality. And then, paradoxically, some of the old desires and beliefs may jump up again, and you wish they wouldn't, because you can see how they disturb your peace.

Now everything is not lost, nor does it all stay melted. Like the ice cap that melts, it reconstitutes itself in some ways. But what is needed is to find out what is truly authentic for you – in relationship, work, and lifestyle. It is unique to each person, including some of the old ways and some that are new. If you are in a process of spiritual awakening, you are forced to live an authentic life, or you will be miserable, perhaps even ill. Usually patterns you followed that were driven by ego can no longer be sustained. There is no more room for lying to yourself about how you are going to express yourself in the world, and there is a deep interior impulse to move in new ways you may not have considered in your pre-awakened condition.

Many spiritual teachers will say this is so – that they never imagined themselves in the roles they now play, or had any attraction to such roles, when they were doing other work in the world. I was astonished after my kundalini awakening to find myself a therapist specializing in such an obscure topic, and able to lecture without self-consciousness wherever I was invited. In no way could I have imagined this five years earlier. But it was obvious it was where I belonged at that time.

Dark Night of the Soul

Most people in spiritual circles have heard about the "Dark Night of the Soul", a phrase first expressed by the Christian mystic St. John of the Cross. There can be many reasons for this experience during a kundalini awakening (or any other spiritual process). Primarily it is felt because of this falling away of the familiar identity, so that one loses zest for life, temporarily, or feels empty of drive and direction. We become habituated to functioning in a certain style and do not know what to do when those old drives are gone. The mind tends toward depression at such times.

Another factor is that after an ecstatic awakening it often happens that in a few days or weeks or months the blissful aspects fade, and it seems that the most wonderful blessed state of consciousness ever known has been lost. Great despair can set in, along with a return of the ego concluding it has done something wrong that caused this falling out of grace. Some people live in despair for quite a long time after an awakening, primarily because they get stuck in a new identity which is less functional than the old one, and they do not know how to move on.

If you find yourself in this condition, it is useful to ask two questions. The first is "Who is it that had this experience and thinks they have lost it?" See if you can find that person, that separateness, and you may be surprised. And then go into your heart and ask: "Has that experience of knowing really gone away?" What is here right now at the deepest level of your being? Do not make the mistake of going into memory to recreate the past experience, but rather find out who you are right now, because what is most valuable in awakening is not the phenomena, no matter how grand, but the knowing of who you are without the mind, without any beliefs, without going into the memory of anything you have known. What is living your life in this very moment? These kinds of questions, and the willingness not-to-know are the keys to moving from a kundalini drama into true realization of Self. This realization will eventually free you to move into a liberated life.

The next chapter will cover two remaining special conditions that may cause chaos in a kundalini process: fear of emptiness, and memories of childhood abuse.

Chapter 4: Fear and Memory

I woke up one morning with my entire body in a state of fear, and yet there seemed to be no triggering factor -- no thought, no event, nothing happening in the room, not even a dream to tell me why I was afraid. As I felt my way into the energy of this experience I found that it was an energy housed in my cells, as if my nervous system was stuck in a strange vibration that could hardly bare the temporariness of life, as if at any moment the body would be gone. And I could see that aside from the thoughts that generate fear, there is fear in the very DNA, because the body knows itself to be only a temporary manifestation, set up from the beginning for extinction.

I used to think that fear is learned, and indeed the traumas of a young life profoundly activate the energies of fear, which frequently mark us forever after, making us reactive, protective, self-defeating and even violent. Nations create war out of fear (along with greed and attachment to being right). We can be afraid physically, sometimes for good reason.

But the most defeating of fears come from the mind, when we have thoughts about ourselves, our life, or other people that cause us to contract and withhold our vital energies and free expression. It's as if the innate fear in the physical body seeps into the memory banks and distorts our mental perceptions.

We can be afraid of life as much as we are afraid of death, of people as well as of loneliness, of our thoughts and minds, and of the absence of thought. It seems as if there is nothing that someone cannot be afraid of, and that fear lies in wait in our bodies to be brought into action whenever our separate and conditioned identity feels the slightest threat.

So it is understandable that a kundalini process, with its unfamiliar energies and sudden shifts of consciousness, will trigger fear in some people. Often this is expressed as a fear of death or a fear of insanity, neither of which is a probable outcome in the process itself. There are two types of experiences that are especially likely to bring up fear following a kundalini awakening: fear related to emptiness, and physical fear related to early childhood abuse.

Falling Into the Void

I spoke once to an audience of people who had near-death experiences in their history. Most of these experiences are remarkably pleasant, considering the circumstances, with visions of loved ones, lights, angels, or other comforting beings, and ecstatic and loving energies beyond any known by ordinary consciousness. But one woman stood up and angrily told me she had enjoyed no such experience. Instead she had only a voice telling her over and over, "You do not exist!" She felt cheated and wounded by this encounter.

Unfortunately, I did not know at the time how essentially true her experience was. Years later, after a profound awakening to Self, I began to understand the essential emptiness behind all experience. Many people, during a kundalini awakening, fall occasionally into what is called void, emptiness, nothingness, even a kind of blankness or blackness in which the mind is silent and the experience scary. They pop out of it quickly, if they can, and wonder what it means, and they are disturbed by the implications of no self. This is not the spiritual experience they expected, especially if they have been having lovely mystical images and bliss prior to this revelation.

You usually need to go to the scriptures and teachings of the non-dual spiritual paths to find a description of this emptiness that has been stumbled upon unknowingly, although St. John of the Cross alluded to it in his profound writings about his own realization. If you cannot intuitively overcome the fear and enter into this empty space, you will benefit from finding the teachings and recognizing your experience in some of the great systems of spiritual thought such as Advaita Vedanta, and Dzoghen or Zen. If old scriptures seem too remote for you, the teachings of the sage Ramana Maharshi, or some of the modern non-dual teachers may describe the meaning of this territory in more modern language. The important thing is to meet your fear of emptiness with compassion. Release it or move past it if you can, or soothe the mind by understanding what others have had to say about it.

When you have been in a kundalini process, and a deep clearing has been carried out for some length of time, you will be invited into the next stage of awakening, the awakening of mind and heart. These are not experiences of energy as we think of it, but rather openings in consciousness, beyond the energy phenomena. This nothingness or emptiness can also be called vastness, unlimitedness, that which is deathless and eternal.

When you find the courage to fall into it, or you are knocked into it despite your resistance, and you stay awhile, there are great discoveries to be made. Hold still where you are, feel yourself to be *That,* and see where consciousness will take you. No one can speak of this place in language: all words seem to degrade it. It cannot be talked of clearly, but it can be known. Do not let the contraction of fear prevent the openness of being present in this unanticipated spaciousness, simply because the mind does not understand it. This is a place beyond thought, and so the mind and the small self feel threatened. It is a profound invitation into a new territory. But you have to enter it instead of standing there looking at it, and it can feel as if you are letting go of your mind. In this place, true understanding of Self can arise. The sage Bede Griffith, a monk who blended Christianity and Hinduism in an ashram he founded in India, once said that when you enter into this darkness fully, you find love.

Fear Related to Memories of Abuse

Jackie came to me with a story about her sexuality. She had a deep awakening during a retreat, and felt a great opening of her heart, and expansion of consciousness. But when she returned home her sex life had changed. Whenever her husband touched her she would involuntarily experience contraction and physical terror. In her dreams she was seeing a small child being sexually abused. She was very distraught about the impact this was having on her marriage and wanted to transcend it spiritually and move on.

Lauren was a nervous young woman who had been involved in fundamental Christian churches, and she lacked self-confidence, but she went to a meditation weekend with a friend, thinking that meditation could help her feel better about herself. She found it very easy to meditate, simply leaving her body and resting in some distant space, very detached, until suddenly a great energy rushed from the base of her spine into the sexual organs and belly. Everything quivered uncontrollably, she felt intense heat, and her mind seemed to snap. She threw off most of her clothes and ran outside the building and down the street screaming hysterically, unable to control the trembling in her body.

Our bodies store the memories of our childhood, including material that is painful and repressed, which means we do not remember it consciously. If I raise my hand to hit you, you will contract, and that contraction will somehow remain as an imprint long after the physical sense of it is gone. Any therapist who has worked with the body, or with the emotional content of a person who has been physically or sexually abused, has seen how these past events are stored, and must be released for the person to feel free to express themselves fully in the world. People with such histories can certainly lead productive lives, but they often harbor self-doubts or self-destructive beliefs, and they tend to limit themselves unnecessarily due to unconscious patterns woven deeply within.

The spiritual practices in both yogic and Buddhist traditions have a remarkable built-in structure that will ultimately cause the practitioners to release the hidden components of conditioning. In other words, meditation or yoga or visualization can open up all the cells that are storing the memories, and these can erupt to the surface at any time. When kundalini activates this is likely to happen sooner, rather than later, and with an intensity that is shocking. Abuse is stored not only in the cells, but woven into the conditioning, and the memory arises in order to be met, accepted and released from the subtle, physical and mental fields. Remember that the function of kundalini is to make one free, and freedom cannot happen as long as parts of a life are hidden. Consciousness must meet its history in order to free it.

So in some cases unresolved or suppressed memories of sexual abuse awaken along with the kundalini, as it begins its journey from the lower chakras, and the fear and pain of the abuse is felt concurrently with the kundalini energy. It is difficult to open up further and to experience the true potential of bliss when the body is associating the energy with a long-forgotten trauma. In addition, some yogis say that sexual invasion at an early age can cause a kundalini arousal, and the energy will go through the system in a distorted pattern, instead of following the correct channels, and this can cause hysteria, erratic moods, and difficult to control psychological and energetic responses. Later, if a person does spiritual practices the energy will reactivate quickly, because it is already open, but it may charge through the body without much usefulness, destabilizing the personality instead.

In my experience with this phenomena, I have found that it is essential for people with sexual abuse issues, and those with severe physical abuse or other traumatic memories, to receive therapy with someone who has expertise in this particular field, in order to deal with the long repressed childhood story, which was probably never told. It is important to be fully revealed, so that the inner child can finally be heard, experience compassion, and be helped to discover his or her own innate innocence and strength. This is like a preparation for the later work that will naturally be done through the spiritual awakening. There is a need to honor our humanness as part of the whole picture of awakening out of it. To do any less is a spiritual bypass, and will put us in a spiritual cul-de-sac, where we cannot go all the way on our journey to Truth and wholeness.

In the above examples Jackie needed to work through her sexual abuse issues, so that she could restore her sexual freedom with her husband. Her body was telling her the next step in her journey was immediate and personal and about the healing of the separate self. Later she could go more deeply into the spiritual work.

Lauren's case is an example of someone who is not ready for meditation practice, and needs to work through early childhood abuse, and perhaps is better served by a more conventional spirituality at this time. She is too open emotionally, physically and energetically and is not capable of coping with the powerful energies available to her without becoming disoriented. There is a time when having a faith in a higher power, and leaning on that, is nurturing and supportive. Until she has done her psychological work, and found her personal strengths, she is not able to hold the energies that are so easily activated in her body as a consequence of her abuse. This is similar to what happened to many young people in the 60's who had breakdowns as a consequence of drug use. When one misses certain stages of development they are not adequately prepared for the subsequent stage. There are probably exceptions to this perception, but in general this is what I have observed in those who have unusual difficulties with kundalini arisings.

I do not intend to imply that people who have suffered abuse should not follow spiritual practices. Suffering is a great motivator for entering the spiritual path, as the Buddha observed centuries ago. Many who have suffered develop strong characters and a great capacity for truth. They may have compassion for the plight of others, and a hunger to know their true nature. I am suggesting that the more consciousness one has about their history, and the more they have faced it and come to terms with it, the better prepared they are for the events that will occur during the process of psychological deconstruction. Our bodies can open up to an astonishing bliss and peacefulness once the pain is thoroughly released.

Beyond Experiences

You are not your experiences. You, as consciousness, carry an illusory self that believes it is the sum of your experiences, and your reactions to them. The drives, anxieties, sorrows, longings and ambitions that navigate the body/mind through life are energies entangled in the past. They cause you to make the choices you make, and trigger the judgments of self and others that limit your self-expression. Fear is in our physical cells, but it is also an energy derived from many assumptions about ourselves and others, based on our history and experience, and we continually reactivate the cells by exposing them to negative thinking.

When you are able to slip out of the maze of personal history, and live a moment that is immediate and fresh, here and now, free of any need to protect or project any image of yourself, there is a profound internal relaxation. This is one reason many people love being in the wilderness, where there is no one to interact with and only the beautiful acceptance of nature. They can let down their guards and self-consciousness and may discover who they are without them.

Whether you are finding yourself engaged in collecting relative experiences in the world of the body/mind, or mystical experiences that come through the opening of the subtle field, you are neither a human nor a mystic. There is no need to avoid or to seek more experience. You are the spaciousness in which they occur. You can use any label you wish to define yourself in language, and you can play any role that attracts you. But the way to avoid fear and suffering is to discover the spaciousness you are and let it view the experiences you have without the overlay of judgment, demand, attachment and resistance. Most fear and suffering is simply an energy produced by thought, flooding our cells and chemistry. Fear is useful if it helps us extract ourselves from a physically dangerous situation. Pain is inevitable at times as long as our vehicle is a physical form. But most of our fear and suffering is inflicted by thought, and amplified by DNA and memory.

When fear arises in your spiritual life, it will transmute if you will embrace it as an energy that is telling you that you are close to falling into Truth. You might put more attention on asking who you would be without this fear. What is it that notices this energy? Is it an image in the mind, a mere thought, or is it Truth that is stimulating this energy called fear? We do not need to allow the habit of fear to dictate our lives, for if we do, our lives become a mere shadow of their potentiality.

One of the insights of living in the present moment, instead of the memory of the past or a fantasy of the future, is that you realize that nothing fearful is happening right now. If it were, you would instinctively be responding to it. Fear is often only the energy of the thoughts you carry in the backpack of your mind. Freedom is seeing this fear as an energy that can easily be dropped by the side of the road. Try to be curious rather than afraid.

Kundalini awakening brings many challenges, so it can be helpful to know that as a process it has been recognized for hundreds of years in other cultures. Many have walked this same path. The following chapter will reveal how it is understood in eastern traditions and why many people in those cultures value it.

Chapter 5: The Secrets of the East

For hundreds (or possibly thousands) of years spiritual sects in India and China have followed secret practices developed to awaken the inner spirit, and bring alive the slumbering energy of the life force. In both countries, these have evolved into complex systems, available to almost anyone who asks for them, using many specific breathing and visualization exercises. These are supposed to culminate in a deeply transformative experience through which the student realizes the underlying nature that is shared by all life forms.

Both systems have developed many body/mind practices said to improve flexibility, health, physical and mental strength, power over the elements and other supernatural gifts. However, there is a great divide between the way traditional Indians and Chinese cultures would define and frame these practices. In India, they are part of an ancient and deeply rooted emotional connection to the play of the Divine, and integrated into the development of a long spiritual journey. In China the emphasis is more on clarity of mind, using the energies of nature for healing and well-being, recognizing that we are empowered by our contacts with the deeper streams of energy to which we have access, but rarely recognize until we are trained to do so.

Mystics on the Western Path

Western mysticism is very different from the eastern path, having evolved out of the pre-Christian Judaic traditions, the desert fathers, and the mystery schools of Egypt and Greece, re-framed by the Roman influence on Christianity, and then filtered through the western fascination and reliance on mind that emerged in the Renaissance. Although western mystics describe many of the phenomena that also arise in the eastern mystics, such as visions, enraptured conditions of knowing they are one with God, unconditional love, and insights into the illusory nature of human perception and the oneness of all things, they rarely discuss the physicality of their experiences, other than mentioning pain and suffering.

With no language or paradigm to understand the subtle energies that accompany their spiritual awakenings, the movement of energy rests beneath the surface of the spiritual events Christians may report in their lives. This might account for so many of the reports of ill health among saints and sages in the western lineages, many of whom seemed to experience physical and emotional suffering and even persecution along with the empowerment that accompanied their realizations.

Non-Dual Traditions

Another path has evolved from the non-dual traditions of Advaita Vedanta, and two schools of Buddhism: Dzoghen and Zen. Buddha was born into a Hindu Brahman family, and had followed Hindu paths for many years before he sat under the Bodhi tree and became the first Buddhist. He was steeped in the understanding of spiritual process at that time, because he was already an established teacher with followers, so he must certainly have known yoga meditation and energy practices, and found his way into samadhi, the highest state of unity, where consciousness is merged with universal source. If his greatest insights had ended there, Buddhism would not have been needed as a new approach to spiritual awakening, because there was already an ancient and established path.

Buddhism offered a new perspective, a way to realization through a shift in consciousness and identity, a capacity to drop out of the trance of thought and personal identification, directly into the spacious clarity and awareness of conscious presence with no personal self. It also brought forth a new moderate way to live as an awakened person, and the understanding that awakening was not about acquiring something, but rather the letting go of everything. Satori was the sudden realization of one's true nature as awareness shifted. Both gradual and direct paths of Buddhism evolved as ways to carry this insight.

In this movement, one could be in an alert state of mental clarity, and yet know there was nothing there but awareness, and realize a wholeness paradoxically empty of substance but ripe with potentiality. This was a remarkable discovery in the days before molecular science and the nature of atoms had been revealed. Ancient Hindu teachings understood this universal Oneness too, as is clear from translations of Vedanta scriptures, but Buddha found a more direct method of realizing it.

Some time later, a non-dualistic form of Vedanta was revived by a revered teacher named Sankara, and this offered a direct path through transmission or study with a teacher, somewhat similar in perspective to Buddhism, although followers tended to describe the ultimate experience as a knowledge of Self, while Buddha called it no-self. This approach became known as Self-inquiry after the awakening and teaching of the Indian sage, Ramana Maharshi.

Over centuries Buddhism moved into other countries, merging and adapting with prevailing cultural perspectives in places like Tibet, China, Indonesia, Japan and the United States, and so it now has a variety of forms. Most of them have little reference to kundalini energy, although it is recognized that energy changes happen along with spiritual awakening. These are considered a by-product, and in most systems little attention is given to them, the exception being Tibetan Buddhism, which was melded into Tibetan shamanism in its earliest years, and includes practices for rising and working with subtle body energy, as well as states of calm abiding, and clear mind.

Kundalini Science

In India the study of kundalini energy developed centuries ago, and is a significant part of the yogic and tantric traditions. Because it was studied thoroughly, there are classical texts describing how it moves and affects the human body, mind and spiritual development. India is a vast country and there have been numerous variations over the centuries, so there is little consistency in the practices and methods offered by kundalini masters, tantric practitioners, or numerous other schools of yoga. But it is useful to note the general model that describes how and why kundalini energy moves as it does, because few westerners have an understanding of it, despite the fact they engage in many practices that can awaken it. So this discussion of the science of kundalini is not meant to be a final word, or the only word, on the topic, but may offer some direction for people caught in the experience.

Although there are some correlations with the framework used for Chinese acupuncture, QiGong and Tai Chi, because they also address the subtle body, the elements, and the streams of energy in the body, it is beyond the scope of this book and its author to describe the Chinese system.

Kundalini Science describes humans as existing within three bodies: the physical or gross body, the subtle or energy body, and the causal body. The physical body consists of all that is material, the molecular structures we appear to be, with skin, bones, organs, blood, etc. The subtle or energy body is said to be a network of 72,000 invisible lines of energy called *nadis*, arranged with numerous chakras which interlace it into the physical form. The tradition identifies 36 primary *nadis* and 7 major chakras, and these are of the most interest for someone doing yoga practices, although I have been told by a yogi master there are actually 50 chakras throughout the body, primarily located in the legs. Tantra also describes a number of esoteric chakras extending above the head, which are beyond the scope of my research.

Within the subtle body are 3 finer elemental bodies carrying emotions, thought and senses, and all of our internal activities flow through these bodies. Prana is the term for the energy as it goes through us, and it is fueled by breath. Prana is differentiated into five kinds, said to be responsible for all movements, voluntary and involuntary, such as sneezing, coughing, the circulation of the heart, elimination, sexual action, movement, blinking, etc. Each of the five pranas has a certain directional flow, up or down or circular. Breathing and concentration practices in yoga are used to expand prana, or manipulate it in specific ways to strengthen the body, and facilitate the activation of kundalini.

When kundalini awakens at the base of the spine some yogis say there are six possible energy channels through which it will arise, all within or around the spine. Sometimes awakened energy moves through channels that cannot go all the way to the crown of the head but stops at lower chakras. Optimally the energy moves into a space variously identified either as above or at the crown of the head called *sahasrara,* (sometimes identified as the 7th chakra), a movement understood as essential for realization. If kundalini is caught in one of the lower channels lots of sexual energy can be stirred up. Ideally (but very rarely), the kundalini moves quickly and directly upward through *chitrini* channel. More commonly, it rises through *sushumna,* the central channel within the spine, where it winds upward in stages and can take a very long time to complete. If it is in the wrong channel, kundalini needs to be re-routed into *sushumna* to have a complete fulfillment of its potential. This is accomplished by bringing attention to the base and doing a breathing and concentration practice that focuses on the central channel. The need to recognize errors and route kundalini correctly is one of the reasons that proper guidance from an awakened teacher is emphasized in the tradition.

Sometimes when kundalini first activates in *sushumna* a person may see or feel a streaming of light, smell pleasant or unpleasant odors, or have a sensation of being empty and made of air. There can be many unusual experiences, fearful or pleasant visions, mood shifts and other non-ordinary experiences.

A full arising and completion of this process is considered by yogis to be exceedingly rare. Instead, kundalini energy usually stabilizes in one of the chakras, or bounces up and down through two or more of them. These partial arisings can vary greatly in intensity and produce various phenomena depending on personal tendencies, toxins in the energy or physical bodies, spiritual intention and practices, and general psychological and physical health. Until kundalini has risen and stabilized above the heart chakra, the mind and emotions can be very unstable and erratic.

There are six chakras along the spine and up to a point between the eyebrows (*ajna chakra*). Kundalini can become blocked at any of them, causing specific difficulties and distractions. A few yogis offer specific advanced practices to re-route and break through these blocks, but generally their advice is only accessible to students they are very familiar with, as the practices can be a risk to both physical and mental health when attempted at the wrong stage of the process, or if the body/mind is not sufficiently prepared. Some systems of Kundalini Tantra use sound to open blockages. One set of sounds that help are called the Bij mantras, tones to resonate with each chakra. These can be found on the internet. Yoga asanas (physical positions) and breathing practices can also be helpful, especially alternate nostril breathing, which balances energy unilaterally.

Some of the specific experiences connected with blocked chakras include:

1st chakra, *muladhadra*, at the base of the coccyx. Occasionally there is sharp pain during an initial arising, as kundalini pierces the *sushumna* channel and enters it. There can be itching, pressure, twitching, heat and other discomfort as well, during the early stages of kundalini stirring. A few people have described to me extreme bouts of elimination as if the bowel is being totally cleared in early stages of this awakening.

From this base two other *nadis* (streams of energy) rise on either side of sahasrara, called *ida* and *pingala,* and sometimes kundalini arises through one or both of these. They have been identified as a mental force on the left and a vital force on the right, and also as cooling and heating *nadis*, respectively. Sometimes heat or cold flash through the body if kundalini activates one of these *nadis*. They wind along the spine through the body crisscrossing at each chakra and ending at the 3rd eye. In yoga, an essential practice is to balance these two energy streams perfectly, usually done by gradually developing the skill of alternate nostril breathing. A basic practice to activate kundalini is to balance and suppress the pranas on left and right and then bring them into the central *nadi, sushumna,* which puts pressure on the latent kundalini, forcing it to explode upward. Schools of Kriya Yoga, Ashtanga Yoga and Kundalini Yoga offer other specific breathing and contraction practices to do this, after adequate preparation of the mind and body.

2nd chakra, *svadhisthana,* just above the genital region. The second chakra is close to the seat of kundalini, and in kundalini science it is believed that some kundalini energy is active there after puberty, to facilitate sexual activity and procreation. If all the kundalini energies activate and only move into this chakra, it can overwhelm a person sexually, making them feel crazy and out of control, producing excessive sexual fantasies, even leading to obsessive and deviant behavior. Intense energy here is also associated with anger, fear, and depression. A person may also fall into deep lethargy and want only to sleep. It is important to move the energy upward as soon as possible. In this situation yogic masters recommend having a strong will and fearlessness, along with dispassion, and sincerity in your spiritual intention. For some people initially awakening kundalini may be easy, but they can be stuck in this cul-de-sac indefinitely, because of a lack of understanding, getting caught in a passion to fulfill personal desires, or because they are not motivated to become liberated. Yogis believe this is the point at which one is driven by desire back into the cycle of life and death, or one may break through toward liberation.

Once kundalini is active, the emphasis needs to be on bringing the lower pranic energies into an upward flow, which is a primary reason celibacy is recommended. Sexual activity and orgasm uses a downward-flowing prana, so energy is released that is needed in the upper chakras at this time to facilitate the process. Some yogic systems have even developed ways to end the menses in female yogis, because it is facilitated by a downward flow of prana.

From a yogic perspective, the physical difficulties some people report with heat and pain are related to a failure to manage the prana effectively for the stage they are in, particularly prana related to sexuality. Many westerners who are interested in tantric sex, do not realize that the classical practices of tantra are about turning sexual energy, highly aroused, upward and moving it through the crown, rather than sexual release through the genitals. Most traditional yogic paths do not use sexual forms of tantra (which is a specific school of energy practice) but move energy through meditative and breathing practices. They discourage sexual activity, and if it cannot be contained, students are sometimes advised to go out in the world and satisfy their cravings, before continuing in the process. However, if kundalini has arisen into the second chakra and is blocked there, this would be very destructive advice, and instead, the student needs help to get the energy re-routed and moved into another area. Paradoxically, in a few cases I have met clients who found a sexual release helped them to rebalance and harmonize the discomfort in their energy process. I believe this is an issue to be addressed individually, and choices are dependent on many circumstances.

Some yogic practices are said to convert this sexual energy into a substance called *ojas*, which coats the brain and makes it more receptive to meditation, and supports the arising of energy into the *sahasrara*. Intense headaches and pain in the head during this process has been attributed to a deficiency of *ojas*, so it is considered very valuable to know how to convert sexual energy and move it upward. *Ojas* is also connected to the production of *amrita,* a substance said to release from glands as kundalini penetrates the upper chakras, which causes a sensation of sweetness and ecstasy throughout the body. Some report that it tastes like honey dripping down the back of the throat.

3rd chakra, *manipura,* slightly behind the naval. When kundalini is stuck here there can be digestive difficulties and other stomach problems, and erratic swings in appetite, along with an emotional attachment to power and position in the world. In some ways the belly is the seat of false identity, connected to all the impulses of the lower chakras. It is associated with the need to know one's place in the world, as well as self-expression and power. After the energy moves upward into a full spiritual awakening these drives are muted, and energy may safely return to the lower chakras, bringing stability and creative grounded expression. *Manipura* is the seat of the radiant energy distributed throughout the body so if it is deficient one lacks vitality and when it is awakened one is energized and more available to life. Some Buddhist and tantric texts say the true awakening of kundalini actually happens in this chakra, because after it is fully alive here the energy will not recede again. This is also a place in the body where the upward and downward pranas meet explosively and are believed to fuse and create a new base for kundalini to progress upwards. When this chakra is transmuted personal drives and complexes begin to fall away and there can be a deeper longing to know Truth.

The solar plexus is the area where energies from the upper and lower chakras intersect, and many people have an intense contraction, or dramatic release, even a visual picture or symbol that appears, as kundalini weaves its way through here into the upper chakras. There is also a peculiar condition called Buddha Belly in which some people experience a temporary swelling of the stomach , even appearing pregnant, when energy collects there.

4th chakra, *anahata*, in the spinal column directly behind the center of the chest. When energy is stuck in the heart chakra, which is said to be located slightly to the right and behind the physical heart, there can be heart palpitations and other frightening sensations. There may be pain and accelerated pulse rates, or an intense sensation of burning, or a feeling the heart is cracking open. Some people report a sense their heart has stopped beating for a few minutes, but if they see a doctor they find this is obviously not the case.

There can be a strong intensification of love and compassion. Love of God or a devotional inclination to a guru or saint may arise and absorb a person. Sometimes the love is projected on a random individual, even one who the person would not normally feel attracted to. Many people feel joyful and worshipful when the heart awakens, and there is a shift where one is not so controlled by their conditioning, but has a more broad view of the nature of things with spontaneous and wise responses to life events. Thoughts may seem to manifest into reality and synchronicities occur. Previous drives and attractions may drop away. Sometimes creativity and healing abilities arise. It is important to discard negative thinking because thoughts become more powerful. With stuck heart energy the mind can become unsteady, and a person caught at times in emotional turmoil. The awakening must progress before a person will feel complete, and freed from fluctuations and mood swings.

5th chakra, *vishuddha*, at the throat. It is common for kundalini energy to stabilize for a long time at the throat chakra. This is considered to be a purification center by yogis, where the harmonizing of opposites is believed to occur. At this point a great longing arises for realization and wisdom, for the Truth. Experiences of void and emptiness may occur. There may be a greater resonance with spiritual teachings, an activation of psychic abilities or creative talents, or an ability to speak or write fluently. As this chakra awakens people become more tolerant and compassionate, able to see all sides of life and develop acceptance of the light and the dark. Occasionally they might read another person's thoughts. Some yogis say this chakra is also related to retaining youthfulness, helping the cells in the body to regain the quality of regeneration they had as infants.

On the other hand, until the chakra is cleared some people find themselves with difficulty swallowing, or the neck jerking, spinning or twitching. One person I worked with appeared to have something like Tourette's syndrome, with extreme and spontaneous facial twitching. It appears that many throat blockages are due to the habit of repressing and withholding what we feel and want to say, and to being less than honest with ourselves and others. Many spiritual seekers believe they cannot express anger as it might be harmful to someone, and so in a way they are gagging on it, stuck in the emotions that are hardly recognized, let alone admitted. Some yogis believe that oral sex also damages the throat chakra or leaves toxins that must be released. I have found that encouraging self-expression and release work, or doing gentle neck stretching exercises, along with chanting the bij mantra "haum", allowing the tone to vibrate, helps to open the throat. Continued spiritual practice with deep dedication to Truth, will eventually allow the energy to move on upward. I've also noticed that if I am meditating and suddenly flooded with creative thoughts, my energy is invariably collected at the throat chakra.

The 6th chakra, between the eyebrows. While it is easy to move kundalini into the heart, yogis say it requires long and strenuous practice to bring it into *ajna* chakra, or the third eye, as it is called in esoteric literature. Meditators often report feeling a throbbing in the forehead when *ajna* is stimulated. People who do long meditations on this chakra often become ungrounded and disoriented, as if slightly out-of-body, and their thinking can feel cloudy. They may become attached to glimpses of other realms and come to believe that is the goal of awakening. Once pierced, this chakra produces much of the light and vision phenomena described by mystics. It is also the point where ego identification can shift, sometimes in a great explosion. There are several stages or stopping points in this chakra, according to yoga science, each of which produces a different affect. Some see visions of a divinity to whom they are devoted, some see or feel infused by lights or bright moons or suns. There may be beautiful inner music or sound, insights or psychic revelations. The ordinary mind eventually becomes more still and steady. The activity in the lower chakras becomes inactive. Some yogic systems say this chakra controls all the others, and so concentration here is emphasized. But I have found that extended focus on the 3rd eye without attending to the other chakras causes some people headaches, anxiety, and disorientation. If this is happening it is helpful to bring awareness down into the heart or the belly and ground the energies.

Here is a letter I received from a man that illustrates the difficulties that can arise when someone opens this chakra without proper preparation.

> I've been practicing breathing and mindfulness meditation for a year and was enjoying it immensely. Then I saw a 3rd eye meditation on the web and began to use it. I didn't know what I was in for!!! I suddenly felt a VERY powerful and constant energy stream out of my third eye in the middle forehead and crown. At first it was very pleasurable, but after a short time it became stronger and light seemed to fill my head. I simply panicked and stopped immediately by opening my eyes. Since then I have not been myself, literally. I am super sensitive to sound, anxious, VERY fearful, jumpy and have a lot of difficulty sleeping.

(Like I am scared to do so since I have
been feeling this rise of energy in sleep
and waking at all hours.) My sinuses
are hurting and I have constant
pressure in my head and around my
eyes.

It is impossible to predict how long difficulties
will continue in someone who randomly and
suddenly opens a chakra through an intense yogic or
energy practice without any guidance. Much of the
yogic emphasis on training is related to moving into
this territory gradually. Depending on many
circumstances, eventually the phenomena will either
recede and the body return into balance or the
process will erupt further until it seems to open up
into the space above the head.

In yogic science the final goal is described as
sahasrara chakra, which some see not so much as in
the body, but in the space above, and others say is
not a chakra at all, but a symbol of infinity. At this
point consciousness and physicality intersect, and
when kundalini energy reaches here it triggers the
dissolution of any sense of physical and personal
identification so that Oneness with primal
consciousness occurs. (This does not mean you
never again feel yourself as a body or a person! You
will!)

Although I have not seen it described this way
in yogic literature, it seems to me this movement into
sahasrara is a way of describing the penetration of
the formerly limited personal consciousness into the

causal body, which might be thought of in western terms as soul-consciousness, or pure spirit without identification. Universal consciousness initially moves into this causal form in order to create an experience of life as an apparent separate physical being. Kundalini yoga would call this minute point where manifestation is initiated a *bindu,* and say it is rooted in limitless undifferentiated consciousness. It is believed to be located in the higher cortex of the brain, and when energy touches it we experience the undifferentiated void, and source of consciousness. The theory is that originally it was through *bindu* and the causal body that your subtle body formed, and then the physical form followed as a creation. Spiritual awakening gradually returns our energy toward a direct experience of the causal body, unimpeded by thought forms, and from this body, merging into universal cosmic consciousness is a natural step.

It appears that many of the rare beings who entered cosmic consciousness in the past simply lost themselves in it, never bothering to re-enter the world. For example, there is a story that Jnaneshwari, a great Indian sage born in 1295, authored a treasured version of the Bhagavadgita when he was only 16, then he and his enlightened sister entered into a cave in their early twenties, had the door blocked with boulders, and never came out.

But some yoga systems include a return-process, in which one brings energy back down into the body, enlivened with the light and wisdom of true understanding, making it possible to offer some service to the world. In Buddhism the samadhi or satori realization is seen as a half-way mark, with the true value being a return into ordinary life, recognizing the divinity and wholeness that shines everywhere in the world of form, as well as the formless. This return is called "embodiment" by some teachers. It seems in Christianity, if a mystic touches the awareness of his or her cosmic wholeness it is called Christ consciousness, and the archetype of Christ as being of service to the world is used to inspire Christians to service in the world.

As this process of awakening unfolds in the subtle body it impacts the physical body, the emotions, and even the way one thinks and chooses to live. Whether awakened deliberately or spontaneously, the experience may bring strange sensations, vibrations, warmth and cold, sense enhancement. swings of mood, flushes of insight, and other harbingers of internal change.

If you do energy practices or meditation, you may experience a sense of spirit swelling up within you, blissfulness, restlessness and difficulty sleeping for long periods. You may feel sensitive, as if your skin is thinner, and you may feel ungrounded, as if there is nothing to hold on to anymore. The energy field is expanding and opening and you have to learn to function in new ways to accommodate it. You can stuff it down temporarily by stopping all practices, eating heavy foods, intellectualizing for long periods, or falling into negative moods, but it won't feel as good as allowing yourself to become fully and unconditionally alive. Finally, if you support your unfolding with an open mind and heart, where you may end up is happy, calm, steady and energized, with occasional downloads of bliss and wisdom.

Chapter 6: The Grace of Kundalini

One day when I was preparing a flip board that listed the phenomena related to the kundalini process my daughter, who was home from college, looked at what I was doing and said, "Why would anyone ever *want* to have this experience?" The reader may be feeling this way after reading about the challenges I have described in previous chapters. But despite the startling changes that come with this awakening, most people feel incredibly fortunate that this happened to them in this lifetime. One young man I met was laying in a hospital bed in ICU hooked up to fluids to replace his electrolytes that were greatly depleted after an intense kundalini episode. He looked at his girlfriend, smiled, and said "We are the luckiest people in the world."

The Swiss psychiatrist Dr. Carl Jung once said of a patient who described kundalini-like conditions, that he had never seen anyone with such bizarre symptoms who felt so good about them. Unlike a disease, when a person is more familiar with the phenomena there is often an intuition that what is happening is good and has a creative purpose in your life. Sometimes there are moments of soaring beauty in which it feels like being present in a complete and perfect universe.

While visiting in India I was delighted to be given a copy of a magazine with a beautiful image of a goddess on the cover, and told this was an image of Kundalini. We could think of kundalini as the feminine face of God. There are many god-images in India, because Vedanta sees every aspect of life as an aspect of the divine One, called Brahman. I think of it as monotheistic despite the entire pantheon of gods and goddesses, because there is only one source, out of which everything flows. The masculine forms that are worshipped represent principles, and the feminine goddesses represent their expression in the world. Most male gods have female consorts, because it is through the feminine that the life force comes into form.

Aside from the elaborate mythologies about these gods and goddesses, at the core they represent forces in human nature. Fundamentally Shiva or Siva represents consciousness in its dynamic of dancing in and out of the form of existence, and Shakti or Sakti, represents the energy that came from original consciousness and causes the appearance of form. Kundalini is an aspect of this Shakti, having created us, and coiled itself down at the base of our bodies.

Many people dream of snakes at the beginning or during the kundalini process. The snake is an ancient symbol found in sacred places throughout the world, representing this coiled consciousness. As pointed out in chapter 1, the snake in the Garden of Eden likely represents the personalization of consciousness, the principle that brings us from unified cosmic consciousness into the limited world of identification with form.

Once we have identified with the body and mind (or eaten of the apple of the tree of knowledge), we see everything as duality, and we lose the innocence and joy of living a life in which we trust that everything is okay. We recognize limitation and death. We are no longer of a nature that is just naturally unfolding, but begin to think we have power over it, and vulnerability within it. Perhaps Eve emerged from Adam's rib because pure consciousness was represented in masculine form, and the movement into physical incarnation, into life, was symbolized by the feminine. She ate the apple first because she was the principle of form and creation, and we only partake of the knowledge of opposites because we are in physical forms. Adam has no choice but to follow her way, because consciousness is merged into the forms we live, and follows the imaginings of mind and thought.

Whether imaged as a snake or a goddess this activated energy begins to recreate the interior form through which we engage our lives. Most people who feel her movement eventually notice bliss, even ecstasy. Some describe being drenched in love, shimmering radiance, subtle ever-present happiness, and a peace that passes understanding. A few people have described to me being so overpowered by the sensation of love that they say this is what kundalini is, the overwhelming and unspeakable love that permeates the universe. They may feel this consistently or sporadically for months or years.

To the extent we can surrender, and let it carry us, it can feel like a great shaking out of tension, dropping away all those energies of contraction that have been accumulated in our cells and nervous systems. When this is done, there can be a great fullness that is spacious and empty, like a helium balloon, and we can feel transported out of the suffering that came when we identified with our problems.

In some cases new experiences arise while we lay on our beds, letting this energy run through us. There can be images of childhood, positive and negative, collective scenes of joy and celebration, ancient stories we think could be past lives, light patterns or mandalas appearing in the mind, geometric descriptions of the making of the universe, the appearance of a teacher or god, the smell of sandalwood, or a taste of honey in the mouth. All of these things can be given in this process, none as a result of a demand, and none that can be grasped and held on to later. We may be spontaneously introduced to the vastness of the mind and senses. These experiences are reported, mainly gifts that follow an utter surrender into the process, free of fear, and open to whatever the universe wants to do with us. Here are a few of the descriptions of grace taken from my files.

I had a dream in which a beautiful
man who was full of light came
into my room and made tantric
love to me, and every cell of my
body was radiantly alive. The
orgasmic experience was exquisite,
but he kept saying, "Move the
energy all the way up to your
crown." When I did we melted into
the universe.

***

The most joyous experience of my
life was when I was meditating and
consciousness entered a space of
such profound love it was
unspeakable. I felt completely
wrapped within the arms of this
love and every sense of
separateness from love dissolved. I
was just that.

***

I keep getting this feeling that I
might begin to let myself open up
to this immense love, where I
would love the whole of humanity
unconditionally, just as God loves
through Christ. As if the world is
forgiven in my eyes, and within me
is a fountain of joy so deep and
eternal, so rich and so gorgeous it
cannot be overcome. This feeling

might be growing in me and there
may come a point where I might be
faced with a choice...'do I stay or
do I go'...not literally going
anywhere, but there would be a
sense in which I would walk out
on my life and allow myself to be
more easily overtaken by this
Christ consciousness, receiving
the grace as I feel it in the way
that I think Jesus did. I feel sure
about this but obviously cannot
justify the conviction.

***

At times I would be sitting on the
couch and suddenly fall
unconscious. I never knew what
happened until I was at a
conference at a drumming session,
with my eyes closed, and I
suddenly left my body and felt
myself to be in my kitchen,
watching my son and his girlfriend
sitting at the table. She took her
earrings off and left them there.
Later at home I found the earrings
and called my son who told me
they had been at the house. After
that, I realized that I was astral
traveling in an altered state, and
learned to do this consciously. At
one time I went to my daughter's

hospital bed, put my hands on her
body, and knew I was stopping her
from hemorrhaging. She was
about to lose a pregnancy, but the
bleeding stopped and all was fine.

***

I was driving through town and
heard a voice say, "Go to your
father's home now." I was headed
somewhere else and thought at
first it was just a fleeting thought,
as I had no reason to be concerned
about him. The voice repeated
again, and so I turned around and
got there within 15 minutes. He
had just had a stroke, and I got
him to the hospital.

***

For weeks, wherever I went all I
could see in others was radiance
and love, and my heart was so
open to them. I was never so
happy, and there was just a
lightness of being that is beyond
describing. My son was in a
serious auto accident during this
time and was arrested for leaving
the scene, and sitting in a field a
few blocks away in shock. I went
to the jail to get him out on bail,
and I sat there in peace and

acceptance. He held me and wept.
Even with this my internal bliss
and happiness continued, until
weeks later when I became
bogged down in the challenges of
his time in court.

***

When I read Gopi Krishna's book I
began to doubt that was what I
was experiencing, because he
described a terrible ordeal, and
mostly this was about joy and
ecstasy for me. One night I woke
up to a sound like celestial music,
and a voice distinctly said, "This is
really kundalini. We're just taking
it easy on you."

When I began my research into the kundalini
experience my primary question was, "What is the
difference between someone who has an ecstatic and
wonderful experience with this process, and one who
suffers and can't get through it?" My life work has
been to find ways to point people toward a positive
engagement with this grace and opportunity. Often
medical or pre-existing psychological issues arise
that must be addressed, but what other factors make
the process smoother? Despite many years, and
hundreds of interviews, I have not definitively
answered this question but here are three of the
conditions that I suspect make the experience more

positive: understanding, self-acceptance and preparation.

Understanding the Nature of the Process

It is important to have a context and understanding of this process as a spiritual development that is of service to you. Those individuals who have sincerely wanted an understanding of spiritual truth, or a relationship with God, are more likely to experience grace within this process. Those who have come from rigid spiritual traditions with preconceived prejudices about energy and the body will have a more difficult time because they reject what is happening, or give it some dark and supernatural explanation that prevent them from relaxing into it. Those who have a spiritual orientation that acknowledges the potential for truth and beauty to be at the core of humanness have a much easier time. If religion is exteriorized you feel like something is being done to you by unknown forces outside of yourself, and if it feels bad you naturally resist. When you understand that Truth is part of the *inward* path, that you find God *inside*, then the journey is open to grace. Exterior grace may also descend, but you are not waiting for the arrival of a heavenly outside influence.

Many mystics in devotional states have reported powerful outside visitations, feeling embraced or absorbed in a downward rush of love or ecstasy, and may also report the sensations of being made love to by the divine. These mystical experiences are not the same as kundalini awakening, and usually occur as a response to deeply concentrated devotional states. When they trigger a downward flow of energy, this may in turn activate kundalini. They are not permanent states and can leave a mystic deeply sorrowful when they go away. The inward questioning of who is having this experience is the way to find a permanent sense of grace and peace after having such experiences. Ultimately self-realization is the remembering of what we are.

A Note on Exterior Graces

I believe there are many realms of mind, and certainly many people describe other-dimensional experiences within the kundalini process, or even outside of it, in their ordinary life. Consciousness is boundless, and often we are moved to our spiritual life by an unseen force that appears as a vision, a miracle, or an unexpected shot of grace. Sometimes a divine person, or a guru or teacher appears in consciousness to help direct the experience. At other times a dream, or an encounter with nature or even a unique stranger opens us up. Perhaps the difference between a mystical or other-dimensional experience, and a kundalini or spiritual awakening, is that in the former the other-dimensional event seems to come from outside of us, while the latter seems to occur within.

Consciousness is both within and without, the form and the sustenance of all life. We have access to realms the relative mind cannot imagine, until they appear in our perceptual range. Sometimes we are invited into a spiritual journey through these external manifestations because they disarm our ordinary way of thinking, and suggest to us there are more possibilities in life than the culture has admitted to.

These super-normal experiences sometimes occur during a kundalini awakening, or occur in ordinary life long before such an awakening. They are not essential to self-realization and it seems that some people are just more accessible than others to these expanded dimensions. Despite the pleasure of such graces, it is useful to return to the inward path. Finding who it is that is having these experiences, and anchoring that wisdom in your physical body, will allow you to move toward a natural awakened life, instead of having an ungrounded disembodied sense of living in the magical realms, longing for repeated phenomena, and resisting the human experience.

The Capacity for Self-Acceptance

Those who have had psychotherapy under the guidance of someone who has helped them learn to witness their own shortcomings and history until they achieve a relative dispassion, are much more prepared to navigate the challenges of a kundalini awakening, and be open to the benefits. Our true nature, the consciousness within us, has a tendency toward compassion, wholeness and love. Nothing is excluded. It accepts all parts of us. So those parts that are dark and painful in our personal and collective minds must somehow be met with compassion, instead of fear, rage and guilt. When we learn to accept whatever is, we are moving toward genuine freedom, and the process unfolds more gently and completely. Along with becoming more tolerant of bizarre symptoms it is helpful to forgive oneself and others if you are stuck in a difficult place in this process,

The Dalai Lama once told a group of Western students that he was astonished to find so much self-hatred in students here. Our culture, imbedded in competitiveness rather than cooperation, tends to leave childhood residuals of self-doubt, a sense of inadequacy, and deeply ingrained interior critics in our psyches. While our ego is simply the movement of mind that identifies with our thoughts and experiences and thinks these represent who we are, our super-ego is like a torturing overseer who has many judgments about the quality of our thoughts and our behaviors, and can be especially harsh on those who see themselves as "spiritual". This is not a service to the awakening of Self or wisdom. We do not become self-realized through judgment, self-condemnation and forcing ourselves to be better behaved. We only become more enmeshed in the delusions of our conditioned personality patterns. In these cases the kundalini energy not only has to clear out the conditioned patterns, but the overlay of judgment and negativity. We can feel overwhelmed as all these pieces come forward in consciousness, one by one, to be seen clearly.

We can become more grace-prone when we are able to be open and vulnerable, as innocent as we were as children, before any judgments ever fell upon us. We were only openness, love and presence then, and we still are, but these overruling thoughts of a separate self who is a problem keep us from remembering this.

Awakening When the Body/Mind are Harmonious

Yogic systems, and some Buddhist schools, have traditionally placed a great deal of emphasis on preparation before kundalini awakening. Only those with healthy personalities, and great dedication to awakening, were allowed into the system in the first place. Then preparation involved purifying the body through complex cleansing practices, breathing practices that open the subtle body, physical practices that make the body more flexible and open, and lifestyle practices that tend to make life more simple and peaceful. Devotion or service to the guru or to others was emphasized to make the ego less assertive. Students were discouraged from using alcohol or recreational drugs, eating meat and sometimes other stimulating foods. All of these conditions tended to make the student more physically harmonious, long before doing practices that might stimulate kundalini.

Very few westerners who activate kundalini have had this preparation, and instead most of us come into awakening with many bad habits. We eat and drink whatever is before us, sleep erratically, stimulate our minds with heavy crime shows, horrific world news, and horror films, live with stress in our personal relationships and our work situations, and use drugs to calm ourselves down or pick ourselves up. Sometimes there is heavy abuse and drama in our history, or a latent illness we have not treated adequately. Our bodies and minds are not prepared to be innocent and open, blissful or peaceful.

It is not impossible for grace to suddenly descend in the midst of all this stress, and occasionally a person is knocked over, like Paul of Tarsus was knocked off his horse on his way to war, and wakes up a different person. But then there is a great call to change your ways. Presumably Paul did this, as he later became a preacher and saint, or he might have had a very difficult time of it.

For this energy of kundalini to bring peace to the receiver it is most helpful to have a calm and receptive disposition, a healthy body, a stress-free lifestyle, a drug-free energy field, and mellow friends. The practices that will help this process move more gently in your life are discussed in a later chapter.

Aside from these issues, there is no guarantee that you will feel graced by the kundalini experience, and a few people appear to suffer with many powerful difficulties that are triggered by the intensification of energy in their bodies. However, it is very rare to be made permanently ill, and in most cases it certainly is not the nature of kundalini to do so. When illness happens it is likely an underlying physical or emotional imbalance that has been amplified by the energies.

More commonly kundalini simply triggers a string of odd and sometimes uncomfortable events, and they pass as the energy moves up and through the crown, bringing realization. This may take a few hours or 25 years. Usually the most intense experiences are in the very beginning weeks and months. Yogis would tell you the degree of difficulty depends greatly on your previous life preparation, your readiness in this life, your personality style and whether or not you have the assistance of someone who has already completed the process. Other factors I have noticed are the general state of the energy system, the health in the past history, the level of emotional maturity, and the capacity for self-witnessing.

Even though there are no guarantees, the opening of a body/mind usually does bring grace. To know the unlimited and eternal vastness of the pure mind, and the universal wholeness we all share, is wondrous and life-changing. To feel our minds as open and radiant expansiveness, free of attachment to thought for even a few moments, brings great happiness and peace. When cells break free of the contraction of lifetimes there can be ripples of great ecstasy flowing through the energy field. When we no longer care how life works itself out, not because the heart is closed but because it is open and trusting, there is indescribable equanimity. This allows us to move spontaneously toward what is needed in the moment. These are the true graces that flow from kundalini awakening, once it has come into its full flow. In time, if there has been a drama, it will subside. Our spiritual journey will regain its footing and follow on into the more mundane aspects of life.

Chapter 7: Nurturing the Process

Kundalini awakening has been called a purification process. In yogic terms this is the release of *samscaras* and *vrittis*. *Samscaras* are all the conditions brought into this unique life to be played out from previous lives, but also included are the consequence or effects of choices made in the present life. *Vrittis* are all the internal movements of mind and thought. Many spiritual practices exist for the purpose of calming and overcoming the activity of the mind, breaking old patterns, and clearing psychological conditions related to *samscaras*.

Deconstruction of the Past

This process is about deconstruction. It gradually strips away old identifications that were woven through your energy field in this and previous lives, including everything you have learned to think about yourself and others, and tendencies that have probably been brought through genetically. When the awakening of kundalini is completed you will likely have some of these tendencies, preferences, and thoughts as well, but you no longer will attach importance to them. They are arising from a field of spacious emptiness and will return there, and you will experience yourself as that field; that is, if any sense of self-experience can be attributed to this at all. You will continue to live in the world in a way that looks like everyone else, and you may be drawn to engage in some activities, but you will experience a freedom from self-identification with who you are and what you are doing.

Because we are spirit imbedded in a physical body, all of the cells of our bodies are like parts of a hologram, containing the memories of whatever has happened to us. So it happens that as the energies that intend to transform us move through the body, any areas where energy, pain, memory, or contractions are stored will react. This is what we are feeling when there are pains, jerking movements, heat, vibrations, rushes and other phenomena during and following a kundalini arising. Our subtle field is opening and coming undone, and preparing to be rewired.

Opening the Chakras

Many people have associated kundalini movements with opening the chakras, which as described in Chapter 5, are part of the classical subtle body model used in India to describe how as contraction releases, old patterns drop away and new possibilities emerge. These energy vortices where the subtle, physical, and causal bodies intersect are where memory, sensation, thought, emotion and

consciousness merge. Each chakra is believed to
carry specific tendencies and to be blocked by certain
reactive contractions and patterns. Generally, the
chakra at the base of the spine is associated with our
foundation in the world, our sense of stability in
being here. The second chakra is associated with
sexual energies and impressions, the third with
power and a feeling of capability in the world, the
fourth (near the heart) with love and receptivity, the
fifth (in the throat) with verbal and creative
expression, and the sixth (between and above the
eyebrows) with intuitive awareness.

There are extensive writings that place
psychological or esoteric meaning on chakras, and it
is beyond the scope of this guide to explore all the
nuances and philosophies regarding chakra change
and transformation. (Books that discuss chakras in
more depth are included in the book list at the end of
this book.)

Various spiritual systems focus on specific
chakras, such as the base (to open kundalini
energy), the heart (in the Self-inquiry taught by
Ramana Maharshi) and the sixth (also called the
third eye), which is believed in some yoga systems,
and some western esoteric practices, to be the
primary modulator of all the other chakras, and the
doorway into other-dimensional experience. In my
observation the kundalini energy can manage the
changes of the chakras quite effectively without
much help from us, if we will only relax, and
surrender to the whole process of deconstruction or
getting rewired, which is how it often feels.

If energy seems stuck in a particular chakra the tension can be released in several ways. Often it is helpful to simply move attention to another area, because energy tends to follow attention. So if there are headaches or chest pain, gently bringing awareness into the belly can balance and harmonize the system. Feel the belly open and expand with each breath, and allow the energy in your lower body to move and come alive. If the second or third chakras are over-stimulated, imagine a wide transparent tube running from the base of your spine to the crown of your head, and let your energy flow upward into the heart or higher, flowing gently up and down as you breathe. With each inhalation let the energy move up and with exhalation back down again. Increase the width of the tube until this is comfortable. Relax your breath, and use your imagination to create spaciousness within you.

If the throat chakra is blocked (a common condition) try singing, roaring, deep humming noises, or other sounds and look for areas in your life where you are restricting your expression, and begin to tell the truth. Spiritual seekers often get stuck because they believe they cannot express anger, and so feelings become knotted in the throat. Finding a safe way to release what you really feel can help unblock the throat and the heart.

There are yogic asana (or movement) practices to open the body, and sounds or tones called Bij mantras, mentioned earlier, that can relax and expand the contraction of blocked chakras. Some spiritual systems use visualizations along with breathing practices to accomplish this expansion, for example sitting in a meditative state, and consciously moving your breath into each chakra as you inhale, beginning at the base, and then, as you exhale, imagining the breath moving upward gently to the next chakra, until each is energized and open. You can learn some of the asana or breathing practices techniques from a person who teaches Ashtanga or Raja yoga. Kundalini yoga also teaches stimulating breathing practices, although they may be overwhelming for someone who has already activated kundalini energy. Gentle healing forms of QiGong or Tai Chi can also be helpful. I especially like Wild Goose Qigong which is done with gentle flowing movements. There are gentle hands-on body treatments such as acupressure and Amma massage that open up energy using pressure points on the body. Cranial-sacral work is a specialized treatment on the head done by some body therapists that can also relax and open up the energy patterns that may be blocked. A general rule in exploring energy practices is to evaluate how you feel later, and stop doing things that over-stimulate you or cause discomfort.

Sometimes when energy is consistently stuck in one place, causing pain, it is related to a psychological contraction, or even an apparent other-life experience. In such cases this is a call for some psychological counseling or perhaps past-life regression work, to release a knot or unconscious memory. People are sometimes surprised to discover psychological issues arising in the spiritual process and hope to bypass them with more meditation or by experiencing liberation. But in many cases these issues must be addressed on the relative level, in order to facilitate the clearing process. If we want to move through this process in a healthy way it is important to respect the needs of the body/mind that has brought us into it.

People carry their pain in different ways, just as we live our lives in different ways, and so there can be a wide variety of responses to this movement of energy, or clearing. Everyone has a specific personal pattern related to which chakras are more or less functional. If there are physical problems from an old injury there may be areas of the physical body that are especially sensitive, and it can feel as if kundalini energy is concentrated to do repair work there. If our diet has been unhealthy or our lifestyle causes us to live where there is toxic emotional energy, this can leave us more vulnerable to difficulties in the emotional component of the subtle field, subject to greater fluctuations of moods. If there has been abuse of any kind, or there is a history of alcoholism or drug-use, the body may be especially challenged to release residual contraction and/or toxins during this awakening. Tolerance and patience is demanded. If there is a tendency toward contraction, and a strong desire for control, the process can be very difficult because of concepts and fears about losing control and habitual resistance.

There is an old saying , "What one resists, persists," that seems especially true during a kundalini experience. Imagine the freedom in your life if you completely released that knot in your belly that wants to be in control, trusting you can respond appropriately to whatever arises without planning ahead.

General Guidelines

Here are ten basic guidelines that can help you move through this experience. Notice, I do not say you can integrate this experience. You can't, and the attempt to do so only makes it more difficult, because it is an effort to put the mind in charge, and this process is much greater than mind, so you cannot control it. When the kundalini has done its work and your awakening becomes more about consciousness remembering itself, then your life is integrated or dissolved into *it*. This will be explored more fully in The Awakening Guide. At this stage the task is to learn how to dance with the unruly new flows of life that are surging through your body. Here are the ten guidelines.

1. The energy may feel coarse and intense at times. But it is rarely painful. Usually it is the fear and the attempt to stop it that causes pain; sometimes, it is just an inevitable stage of the work. If you are having lots of body movement, lay down once or twice a day on the bed, and invite the energy to move through you and clear out whatever doesn't belong to you, and whatever is in your best interest to release at that moment. Usually you might shake involuntarily, or feel waves of vibration running through your body, for just a few minutes -- maybe up to 20 – until it stops, and you will feel more relaxed. You especially need to do this if you work in

an environment where you may be picking up negative energy, or the pain of others, such as in hospice or hospitals, healing or therapeutic work, or where there is a lot of alcohol use.

If you are having persistent physical pain in this process you should have a medical evaluation. The rushes of energy can easily cause metabolic imbalances, hormone or electrolyte disturbances, potassium deficiency, over-stimulation of adrenal or thyroid glands, over-activity in the nervous system, digestive disturbances and other problems. Usually these pass, but medical care (especially if the thyroid or adrenals are not functioning properly), or consultations with Ayurvedic practitioners, can help to restore balance to the system. (It is not likely to stop the energetic phenomena.) As discussed earlier, Ayurveda is the holistic medical system that comes from ancient India and is still practiced today. Some doctors of Chinese medicine also know dietary and herbal methods of harmonizing energy. If there are consistent headaches, a common complaint, it is useful to assess your diet and stressors to identify any factors that contribute to them, learn to move energy downward into the heart area, reduce stress, and spend time in natural settings where you can deeply relax. Sometimes giving up sugar, or gluten, wine or cheese helps release headaches. Do not do concentration practices, especially those that focus on the third eye, if you are experiencing headaches.

2. Discover what your body really wants to eat. Often people need to make major dietary changes such as giving up alcohol and recreational

drug use, avoiding red meat, eating smaller and
simpler meals. If you have a persistent problem with
kundalini, do detective work to see what activity or
habit precedes the problem. How long since you ate
and what did you eat? Would a small piece of hearty
whole grain bread calm it down? Perhaps chamomile
or burdock root tea? Do you need more protein?
Some yogis recommend drinking a mix of warm milk
and ghee, with sugar in it (not honey, which raises
heat), for calming and cooling the energy. Some
suggest dark chocolate after long meditations, to
restore the loss of lecithin in the body.

Another option is to have a good analysis done
with an Ayurvedic practitioner, who can assess your
body type and balance, and recommend the optimal
diet and herbs for you. There is much variation in
what people need to do, and sometimes people have
long periods with no appetite at all, or long periods
with a voracious appetite. Usually a diet focused on
rice, grains and vegetables is most useful, but
proteins are also important. If you tend not to eat
much meat, try a powdered protein and mineral
supplement every day, and add beans and nuts to
your diet. Be good to your body, and eat moderately
or lightly. There is no advantage to fasting, which
can intensify the difficulties. Alcohol, recreational
drugs, and even cigarette smoke will increase toxins
and stress on the body. In times of intense energy
some people report that eating some hamburger or
other red meat will calm things down a bit,
grounding them. Others report that heavy breads
and root vegetables are helpful. It is best to listen to

what your body wants, experiment, and nurture yourself appropriately.

3. Focus more in the heart and the belly than in the head. Look for practices that bring you into the present moment, here and now, eyes open, grounded. A devotional practice such as chanting, or doing a heart-centered meditation, can help the energy open you to an experience of the deeper part of yourself, the eternal part. Service to others or creative expression from the heart can help you move outward into more loving connections, and this keeps the awakening more balanced. If you have a divine image, (a god, goddess, spiritual teacher, saint, or symbol), that is comforting, use it as an ally during this time, talking to him, or her, or it, and asking for support. Some people report that feeling surrounded by light, or visualizing being wrapped in gray silk, seems to calm things down. All of these are powerful archetypal energies that help the psyche when it is moving through challenging changes.

4. Do something to help your body be more open, such as yoga, Tai Chi, dance, acupressure, massage, movement processes, long walks in nature, or whatever you are drawn to. If you don't know what is best for you try several things, and stick with what feels the best. The physical body is the vehicle that will ultimately carry and ground your spirit and awakening. No matter how deep your realization, you will be living in a human body for a few more years. The better it is cared for, the more options you have to express realization when it occurs. However, a person who is weak or dying can also be a

beautiful and complete expression of the Divine, and poor health does not preclude enlightenment. Those who have sat with someone who was dying have seen that as attachment to the body releases, more and more light shines through. There are a few biographies of people who awakened within the dying process. While we are living, having an open and flexible body accomplishes the same thing, with a lot less pain and distraction. Making the body "disciplined" by over-doing exercise is not of any use either. Find a middle way, where your body is in harmony with your spirit.

5. Wake up each day expecting not to know what will happen, and looking with curiosity for the events to unfold. Instead of worrying and controlling, simply be present to whatever arises, intending to meet it fully. Whatever happens in the process of spiritual awakening will be unpredictable and will move on, if you are simply the one noticing it, and not doing battle or making a big project out of it.

6. You may have emotional swings, energetic swings, psychic openings, and other undesired shifts that feel unfamiliar, and foreign to the person you think you are. Be the observer. Don't feel you have to fix or change anything. Recognize that these are natural correlates to awakening and try to avoid becoming either enchanted or distracted by them. They are movements of mind and if you can witness them pass, rather than engaging them, they will move by more quickly.

7. If you have serious trauma in your history, and have never had therapy, it could be useful in releasing the pains of the memories that come up around the events. Many people who report spiritual awakenings have had troubled childhoods. Such experiences often serve as a great catalyst in the search for Truth. I have noticed that people who had good therapy before their awakening often have much less difficulty. Therapy teaches you to express, to witness, to release and to move on. Your therapist does not have to know much about kundalini, as long as he or she does not discount that part of your process. What you want to focus on is releasing issues related to the trauma, and you want a therapist who is experienced and compassionate, and sees your spiritual orientation as a motivation and a support for the process of healing.

8. This process is your opportunity to wake up to your true nature, so begin to explore through meditation and spiritual teachings where this is leading you. Some people wake up first, and then experience a kundalini arising; others have the kundalini process moving through as a preparation for awakening consciousness. The arising occurs to do the clearing out work, so is part of either model, and is not a mistake. Waking up means that you realize or remember yourself as pure consciousness, and ultimately something before consciousness that cannot be defined. You know yourself as a bright, aware, detached and unconditionally loving presence that is universal and eternal, and it is completely free of influence from all the conditions and memories that you associate with as a personal identity.

As long as you believe in your personal conditions and stories, emotions and thoughts, as the definition of who you are, consciousness has to experience life filtered through them. Most humans live far below their true potential because of the false identities they carry. The conditioned mind brings variety and drama to the game of life, but it also causes suffering and fear of death.

We glimpse the Truth about the deep expansive silence that is the ground of our being when we have moments of *samadhi* and *satori.* The early Gnostics called this *gnosis* (knowledge) or the One. Some spiritual teachings, such as Advaita Vedanta and Zen, go directly for the realization, while others see it as a gradual path accomplished through years of spiritual practices. Either way the end is the same. When you know who you are, the world becomes as Shakespeare said, a stage, and you the player, and life is more light and thoughts less intrusive, and the kundalini process settles down into a mellow pleasantness.

9. Give up going places that are stressful and being with people who cause you pain. Sometimes people seem to be more acutely sensitive when kundalini arises. They can't tolerate the energy of large discount warehouses, or smoky nightclubs, or the kind of family gatherings that are tense and competitive. Similarly, promiscuous sexuality brings too much divergent energy into the body. Watching violence in the media may also disturb the energy field. It's okay to take care of yourself and find more quiet time, more intimate friends, and even a new

job, if the old one is overly stressful. Don't feel you
have to prove anything by forcing yourself to be
someone you aren't. Give up the fantasy that if you
are "enlightened" you should be happy wherever you
are or under all circumstances. Rediscover what is
naturally comfortable for you to do, and to be. Live
more authentically. In this process you may also find
a new creative urge, which is a wonderful
opportunity to express what is happening. Draw,
write, dance, work with clay, paint, garden -- all of
these are great ways of nurturing yourself through
the deep psychic changes you are experiencing.

10. Find an awakened teacher to hang out
with. For many people with spiritual awakenings,
meditation is an intrinsic part of their lives. An
awakened teacher will bring you a transmission of
peace, and an opportunity to sit deeply in the silence
of your true nature. He or she can be of any spiritual
persuasion or none, can understand kundalini or not
be interested in it. Seek one who demonstrates
tolerance and compassion, even if they have little
time for idle questions or those who lack
authenticity. Seek a teacher who points you inward
and never toward the adulation of themselves. When
you learn from them the art of sitting and just being,
you will find the cure for the suffering of life. In time
the activity of the mind and complaints of the body
fall away, and there is a deep understanding and love
that arises, which brings a sense of completion,
openness, freshness and an invitation to the
expression of the greater Self. When awakening is
complete, there is no question it has been the whole
purpose of your life. You don't know where it is going

but you no longer care. You surrender to the dance, knowing it is a dream.

The Loving Witness

Have you ever had a moment of stepping out of yourself and seeing your behavior with detached amusement, or surprise? There is a place in us that is always a witness to our lives, but most of the time we are too engaged in the drama to notice this. Some forms of therapy cultivate the witness position, so that you learn to sit in the midst of your own inner division, observing the several positions that your mind might hold, watching its argument with itself. Whenever you are caught between two sides of an argument, notice the witness who is hearing both sides, trying to figure out who is right.

A more deep aspect of this witness is the silence that lies below it. This is the observer who does not make a decision, demand to do the right thing, or place any judgment on the argument. Something has observed every moment of our lives and has noticed how mind tucks away all the memories and images it produces. When we enter stillness or deep silence in ourselves, free of self-reflection, this aware-ing observer is still present. It may be felt as the "I-am", or simply the presence of being. There is an emanation of love from this stillness, a soothing and all-inclusive perspective in which what is happening in this moment is perfectly okay. When it becomes conscious and sees through the arguments, they often fall away, and what is true is revealed.

When kundalini stirs up the drama of deconstruction it is very challenging for the mind to tolerate. But this loving observer can appreciate and embrace this transformational process without difficulty. Through meditation there comes a noticing and cultivating of a relationship with this loving and silent core within us. Ultimately the relationship falls away as we realize this is the core of who we are. When you can sense this open and loving presence within, you have found the place that can hold and appreciate all the varied aspects of the process you are in. Whatever is happening in the external experience of your body and your life, this witness accepts it with compassion and love. Invite it to come alive in your body and your life. The energies of transformation may then become energies of bliss.

Chapter 8: Where to Stand

(This chapter has been available on my website
www.kundaliniguide.com for several years and is
repeated because of the many readers who have told
me it was helpful to them)

I was once delayed for several hours in the
busy and cavernous train station in Florence, Italy,
because I was standing at a track waiting for a train
that never came. All the signs had indicated this
was the right place, and the number matched with
the guide book information, but one by one the
trains came up, indicating they were headed toward
many towns, other than the one where I was going.
Finally I was able to find a station master who spoke
English and I discovered the train had come through
several times, but on a different track. I had missed
the announcements on the loud speaker, all made in
Italian.

Looking back on over 40 years of being a
spiritual "seeker" I realize now that I was often in a
similar situation, standing firm in a territory that
had a lot of activity and potential, but simply was not

headed where I wanted to go. It is not an easy thing to notice, and one would think there would be great humiliation in this discovery. But I have found finally that no matter what meandering path we take to liberation, it is always our own unique and beautiful way to get there. (Or to get to the *nowhere* that is there, because where you are going turns out to be right here!) There may be delays, but they are not mistakes. Although it is humbling, the process is also richly fed by joy and gratitude.

There is a movement from the drama and deconstruction process that takes over our lives after an awakening of kundalini, and sometimes it is so subtle that we miss it. I call it the emergence of stillness. The energy that arises in the activation and continuing process of kundalini awakening could be thought of as our spirit, clearing out conditioning, points of view, old patterns, and all that is held in our subtle body that has helped to define who we think we are.

People have the idea that kundalini is about gaining powers or siddhis, because in India there are practices that appear to lead in that direction, and many openings can happen that allow consciousness to flow in new ways – bringing forth healing, visions, or paranormal and mystical experiences. There is nothing wrong with these phenomena, but they have no value in terms of liberation. They can be used or not used, according to inclination, but if they become new identities, they can delay our awakening to Truth for decades, perhaps even lifetimes. They are distractions that may block inherent peace.

In my work with people who have activated kundalini energy, coming from all stages and conditions of life, I have found few who become enlightened in the process. Many became more wise and loving, or developed new abilities, or simply stayed for a long time in an in-and-out struggle between mystical experience and frustration with ordinary living. And yet in the yogic tradition kundalini is seen as the method, the path to enlightenment. What I have learned in the last few years through working in the Zen and Advaita Vedanta traditions is that kundalini can be considered not so much a goal, but simply an accompaniment to the spiritual process. By this I do not mean it is irrelevant, only that it has a job to do, which is to strip us down to such pure emptiness and openness that the truth of our nature can be seen directly, and lived completely. In the process it ignites and readjusts our energy field, bringing it to a higher frequency.

In yogic traditions that emphasize the activation of kundalini the idea is that by working with the subtle body, doing practices that move this energy up through the chakras, and bringing it ultimately through the crown, one will trigger what could be labeled cosmic consciousness. Some systems suggest one just stays there, sitting in a cave or hut, or even buried in a hole in the ground, indefinitely. But that is incompletion. Other systems teach the awakened to bring energy back down into *hrit* chakra, on the right side of the heart, which will enable the consciousness that is embodied to live a liberated life. This is a useful model, however it is exceedingly rare in the west to find anyone who knows how to do it.

In the non-dual traditions the emphasis is on consciousness. Either through a transmission of presence, or sitting in stillness, or shocking the mind out of its ordinary patterns of thinking, a person can wake up, deeply and profoundly, to the realization of his or her true nature. Actually it is more accurate to say that the true nature wakes up to itself. This is not an event that can be described well from mind to mind, just as one cannot describe the orgasmic experience adequately to someone who has never known it. It is an experience of our very essence awakening to itself, that which existed even before we were born into this body/mind form, with all the conditioning that make us into a unique and illusory personality. To be awake is the goal of the non-dual traditions. This entails a shift of identity from the little "me" into the recognition that paradoxically, "I am nothing – what I am is this vast, unfathomable, pregnant nothingness; and I am everything. What I am is the essence of all of life."

The mind may raise serious objections to this insight, because it seems it will take away the importance of thought, intellect and emotion in ruling our lives, and suggests something else more fundamental is underlying the whole game. And so when there are glimpses of realization the mind quickly rushes into other territory, focusing on new skills, or raising problems, or reminding us of all the limitations we have that mean we can't possibly become liberated in this lifetime. It is so rare to meet a teacher who is actually living from this truth that it is easy to miss its significance even when it happens, because we haven't seen it in anyone else. But in the midst of a great or even a minor mystical experience, and also during an ordinary life event, we can have a flash of that which we truly are, free of all traces of individuality. We are briefly awake, and we quickly forget it.

It is an innocent mistake to believe that if we simply accumulate enough mystical experiences we will be enlightened. These are such awesome moments that the mind places great significance on them. Likewise we may believe that our kundalini process will enlighten us if only we keep working and working on practices, and indeed it does provide us with moments of ecstasy and insight beyond what we knew before it awakened. The mind thinks it knows how to get to the spiritual goal, enjoys the drama of mysticism, and subliminally resists Self-realization because it will mean its own diminishment, so it can keep us in holding patterns for years, even for lifetimes. Also, the fact that we are continually distracted by other attractions in life, or entangled in emotional reactions or intellectual demands, keeps us from having the complete and total dedication to Truth that would lead us into a stable and permanent Self-realized life. Our personal desires and concepts continually reanimate the ego, even after a deep initial awakening.

Often there is a primal core issue or story that blocks completion of our true awakening. For me, I thought it was a fear of love, although I realized later it was also because I did not know where to stand. I could feel there was an opening that happened in truly free individuals who lived not at all for their personal gain, but in service to others, and it looked like love, a love I resisted knowing because I thought it would take over my life and make me painfully vulnerable. For others the core may be a treasured belief system about what they need, what the world needs, or the idea that they are not deserving or good enough to be liberated.

Unfortunately some spiritual systems tell people they need many lifetimes to awaken and take all hope away from their students. This is a great disservice to the Truth, because awakening is always here in every moment, available to every one of us, no matter what the history or core experience of our life. It is rare because so few of us are willing to give up our stance, or belief systems, or personality attachments, in order to see what is beneath them.

To sense directly the awareness that shines through all beings, peers through our eyes, enlivens our senses, empowers our motivations, and carries us through every moment of life, is to take the first step in the radical awakening to Truth which can lead ultimately to self-realization or liberation. We can experience this when we become very, very quiet, in a moment when there is no mental activity of any sort that we reach for or grasp, no practice to do, no idea to uphold. This is the point of sitting meditation. It is not that we reject the world, because rejection is also activity. We simply move into the silence, the deep stillness that is underneath all form and all movement, in the same way that the sky holds all planetary forms and every other part of existence. This is a consciousness that pre-exists, always exists, and never stops existing, and our personal lives are superimposed upon it. To wake up is to know oneself as That. Jesus said it as, "I am that I am"; the Non-dual sage Nisardagatta said it as, "I am that"; Ramana Maharshi, the great sage who taught Self-Inquiry, said it, "There is only the Self"; Buddha said it, "There is no self." When asked if he was enlightened, he simply said "I am awake!".

In yogic systems kundalini movement is a long and challenging process that may eventually lead us to this realization. In non-dual teachings waking-up happens first, and then kundalini will likely happen simultaneously or follow in the wake of this shift into awakening, beginning its work of deconstructing the persistent self-identity.

I have seen many people wake up these past few years, while sitting with my teacher Adyashanti, who awakened in the Zen tradition, and now teaches outside of all traditions. And I notice that after the initial waking up, which may be very brief, or very deep and profound, the person finds himself or herself shifting back and forth, in and out of old identifications, even though they know these are not true. They see clearly they are the One, as well as the Whole. They understand there is no personal "me" other than the energies of conditioning that have been superimposed over the One, but the mind keeps reentering the life, bringing up old issues with brilliant clarity, activating dormant emotions, and stimulating great doubts. So in the non-dual tradition the process of living from that which is liberated happens after the initial Self-realization. (And no little "me" ever gets liberated; its importance simply fades away once it has been truly seen through.) It happens as we stand and face all the fragments of our so-called individuality and let them burn away, so that what is underneath can shine through.

So to fulfill the promise of a kundalini process the consciousness must recognize its own Self as the One Self, and this involves giving up the illusion that mystical experience is the Way. Usually the power and drama of a beautiful mystical experience overwhelms the emotions, and we come back longing for more and more of this. The problem is the continual reconstitution of the person who longs for more. In the excitement we forget to ask who was having the experience, or what is it that has the experience. It is the same One that has all experiences.

When we know absolutely that we are only that which is presence, in this moment, open and awake, then we find there is no longer any hunger for mystical experience, no longing for realization, no more "seeker" and no more objection to whatever arises in our lives. Kundalini may rage through us and we assume whatever is happening is okay. Kundalini may stop its continual gnawing at our subtle field and become quiescent and we just enjoy the peace of it. A mystical opening may occur and it is pleasant. No mystical experiences happen and life is still good. The one who was in the middle, the little "me" who thought things should be a certain way, has stepped aside.

When awakening happens we can become lost in space for a while, enjoying the leap into emptiness and the sense of who we are without any of the limitations our mind had placed upon us. We feel expansive. Compassion and unconditional love may awaken, because our true nature naturally expresses this way. We might feel we can do anything, although this tends to be spiritual ego leading us down a high-risk path. It is true in an absolute way, because at the absolute level we are indestructible and One, but not necessarily true of the bodies in which we carry this realization. To dance in this vastness without any sense of boundary is not the whole of freedom however, because if we can only be free in space we are not free.

So the completion of this journey is a return into ordinary life, and the discovery that the light and spaciousness of the whole is reflected in a myriad of ways in form, and seeing the delight and play it enjoys in those forms. The pain and anguish inherent in the limited life is also clear, and one realizes that the limitations of a world lived through the mind's belief systems are dualistic and thus promote conflict and fear.

When the mind alone rules life it is completely self-centered. This is not a judgment but an observation – mental patterns center around the individual selves, or in some cultures, the cultural selves. That is why people with divergent ideas, beliefs, theologies, financial status, political stances, etc. come to blows so often, and are even willing to kill to protect opinions, and differences. When people are fully awakened they can no longer take on self-righteous positions, because they see through the limitations of mind. So realization is not about creating a more brilliant mind, but discovering a deeper wisdom, one that comes through the heart and has no investment in being right. It becomes a way to live that is simply flowing with what seems to be arising in the moment, a responding, a natural meeting with what is, a blending of love and wisdom. To the mind this sounds impossible, even dangerous. But to the heart it is clearly a reflection of the ancient teaching "Thy will be done."

Kundalini awakening is a great opportunity to become fully conscious to who you essentially are, and to find yourself at one with all beings. The completion of this process is not what the mind would think. Adyashanti says in working with hundreds of students he has never had anyone say to him "This feels just the way I thought it would." That has certainly been true for me, because I now see I stood at the wrong track in the station for years, entranced by my love for the ecstasy of the kundalini energy, and my mystical experiences.

Many spiritual seekers are trying to escape this ordinary world, and do not realize the great gift of returning to it as a whole person, finding no difference between the profound and the profane, seeing God in all of it. Sometimes God is blinded by delusion and sometimes God is experiencing great congruence, but it becomes more and more obvious nothing else is happening but God having many experiences. One of the Zen sutras puts it, "Form is emptiness; emptiness is form." All One.

To become whole we embark on the great process of being stripped to the core, seeing all our patterns and all the darkness of the world as well, arising inside of us. There is waking up to knowing "I am this" just as in the foundational Indian scripture, "The Bhagavadgita", Krishna (divine Beingness) shows Arjuna (his human disciple) his true face, and Arjuna cannot bear to look for more than a moment. The little "me" cannot sustain this understanding, but the greater Self that we discover we are, can hold it all, and is already holding it all. That is what leads to liberation, the absolute willingness to hold it all, and then when the timing is right, to live as that, to give up the boundaries of being self-centered, and ask what is that which wants naturally to be expressed through me. It will be different for each of us, according to some unique divine plan that no one has access too, but there will be an expression.

We can't decide to do this with mind and it is not a practice. It just happens when we let awakeness run its course. Certain old traces of the humanness may object, just as Jesus asked the cup of crucifixion to pass from him, but in the end it will be done, graciously and with no attachment to the outcome. We begin to flow with the impersonal consciousness that lives this multi-faceted life of human existence.

This is what I have learned finally, after many years, and after giving up the search. Because it was so important for me to know where to stand, I find myself passing this along to you. Wherever you have stood it has never been a mistake, but may you be blessed to discover along the way just who it is that is having the experience. That essence that is the real Self is here right now, in the middle of the kundalini process, and before it, and after it. Just become wordlessly and profoundly still and you will discover the mystery you are, and know that you are One.

Chapter 9: Questions & Answers

Over the years of responding to people who have awakened kundalini, I have received every imaginable question about this experience. This chapter addresses fifteen of the most common questions and concerns.

What can I do to awaken kundalini?

There are several schools of yoga that offer gradual programs said to awaken kundalini energy over a period of time, and many people who follow meditation or energy practices sincerely on other spiritual paths such as Buddhist, Sufi, Subud, Quaker, or contemplative Christian paths have a potential for this energy to awaken.

Kriya yoga, tantric practices, kundalini yoga, ashtanga or raja yoga, yogic practices that work with sound or breathing, and many other schools provide systems of preparation for this awakening. QiGong and some martial arts systems can cause an awakening, and so can therapeutic breathwork such as Psychotropic Breathing, or Rebirthing, although these can be overwhelming for some people. New age teachers offer workshops where intense practices, fasting and altered states are experienced for the primary purpose of activating kundalini. Esoteric schools, shamanic exercises and psychic training programs may also trigger energy arisings, and also being in the presence of a teacher who is awake, or intimacy with someone who has strong Shakti emanating from their presence. (Do not assume strong Shakti means someone is self-realized. The energy can and does operate independently of the deeper wisdom of Self-knowledge.)

The challenge in all of these systems is finding a facilitator, mentor, guru or teacher who recognizes the implications of activating kundalini energy, knows it is more than a "feel-good" process, and realizes that it has a powerful capacity to deconstruct the psyche. Even though the energy could be said to know what it is doing, you will not know, so it is a great help to have a teacher capable of guiding you through the process. Some systems, such as breathwork, may work quickly to implode the energy within, but have no teacher available who is awakened and able to guide a person into the peace of completion. Some teachers have the misguided perception that no problems will ever occur with a kundalini activation, and so they frighten the student if this happens. Others turn the awakening into a new ego identity embracing power, or the manipulation of others. Some are just naively enthusiastic, passing along methods and opening up people with no idea of the psychological and physiological havoc that may follow.

The question is, are you prepared for an awakening? Why do you want it? If your intention is simply to activate a dramatic energy change, you may find yourself in great difficulty after this sudden awakening occurs, for it is not a casual event. It is far better to engage in a sincere meditative practice, with a teacher you trust who leads a harmonious life, and to let the seeking of Truth be your guide. Then, when awakening occurs, it is a natural flow out of the sincere intention and development of your practice, occurring perhaps even after an experience of realization of Truth, and your life is already oriented to the perspective it will bring.

At this time (2014) there is a program in India known as the Oneness University that offers through transmission and practice what the founder considers a series of awakenings, and people who attend (I've heard there are over 1.8 million at this date) are "certified" awakened to some degree or percentage. (An oxymoron in more traditional circles, which say it would be like saying you are a little bit pregnant.) It does not deal specifically with kundalini to my knowledge although some who return home go into this process, without guidance. In my observation some come home with a deep realization and others are passing along transmissions with little awareness of the depths of process they may be triggering in others. I mention it because of the great numbers who are attracted to it. Such movements hold both the risks of delusion and ego-enhancement and the potential of realization.

What should I do about this awakening?

Learn about the process, learn to trust it, find ways to ground and make your life as ordinary as possible. Follow the guidelines in this book. And then do as little as possible! Do not let the mind take over with a lot of rules and expectations. You are not in charge here. Give in gracefully. Learn to be a witness to the unfolding, and rest in the pure consciousness -- the awakeness that is your core and exists before thought, judgment and deliberate action. Seek out an awakened teacher to inspire you. Take care of your body and do not indulge in fear.

Is this contagious?

Yes. All of us pass our energy around all the time, no matter what our energy level is. Think how your body feels when you are with someone who is depressed, or with a person who is laughing hysterically. When kundalini is awakened in you, you can feel it in someone else. You can receive a shakti transmission from another person, and you can inadvertently give it to someone else who is sensitive and receptive to you. This is not to say this is likely, only that it is possible. Your lover is particularly vulnerable to picking up this energy, but it may be felt more like a passing of energy through them, and disturbances in their energy field. It does not mean their own energy has awakened, only that their pranic systems are reacting to you. They may or may not like this. You may also find that if you get massages or other hands-on work, your body will start jerking, shaking, or running energy intensely, especially if you relax and allow it. So if you get body therapy it is wise to forewarn the practitioner and make sure they know it does not hurt you, and find out if they are up for it.

What do I tell my family and friends?

People who have never experienced kundalini are unlikely to understand what you have to say about it. Use simple language, such as telling them your yoga or meditation practice, or whatever else is the source, has caused a lot more energy or heat to run through your body, or a lot of memories to surface. Find simple ways of providing just enough basic information so that they are not surprised at your complaints, and not alarmed by your condition. If you do not make a drama out of it, neither will they. I had three teenagers at home at the height of my kundalini awakening, and a husband with a conservative professional career. I discussed it with knowledgeable people outside of the home.

Why doesn't my doctor or therapist know about this?

Doctors and therapists cannot diagnose anything outside of their paradigm. In other words, if it wasn't in the training and they never knew anyone with the experience how can they be expected to recognize this obscure eastern phenomenon in you? Some are more open than others because they have followed eastern spiritual practices, or done some reading about it. In very recent times, a non-pathological diagnostic category for religious or spiritual crisis was included in the diagnostic manual used by therapists. This was originally intended to represent this condition, and motivate the education of therapists regarding it, but the description was watered down extensively by the respective psychological schools that created the manual, so that it is unrecognizable. It is primarily used for crises of faith, or understanding ethnic and cultural variables in spiritual beliefs. Some day the originators of this diagnostic category have hope it will become more inclusive.

Am I crazy? Is this the same as psychosis or bipolar disorder?

There are many factors that distinguish spiritual awakening from mental illness, although it is possible for the two to occur simultaneously, because if there is a serious underlying disorder it may be amplified by the arising of energy. The major difference is that in a mental disorder there appears to be an underlying problem of structure in the psyche: that is, the thinking or emotional states have never been in balance in such a way that a satisfactory lifestyle, work, or relationship can be accomplished. Usually, such disorders show up in adolescence or early adulthood, and if you look at the life history you can see that certain patterns of functioning have just never worked smoothly for the person. There may have been much confusion over which thoughts are real and which are imaginary, a paranoia under circumstances that most people would not consider threatening, poor impulse control, mood swings that seriously disturb relationships, or unresolved addiction, behavioral and abuse issues that suggest an underlying personality disorder. These issues are less common in people with spiritual awakenings who, although many of them may have led unconventional lives, are usually people with some degree of stability in lifestyle, relationship, completion of educational goals, capacity for insight, cooperation and control of impulses. They come from every walk of life, such as students, homemakers, professors, doctors, judges, business owners, scientists, ministers, therapists, nuns, teachers, salespersons or secretaries. They are usually well educated. They are often alarmed about their sanity when they have initial openings because they recognize that their experiences are out-of-the-ordinary. If they have never read eastern spiritual literature or transpersonal material they may have no paradigm for the transpersonal experiences they are having, and mistakenly relate it to the world of psychological illness. They are not confused about the fact that their minds are acting in different ways, only concerned, and they remember well how their functioning worked before the awakening.

Does this mean I am enlightened?

"You" will never be enlightened, whatever you think this means (and everyone has a different idea). You *can* go through a process in which the separate sense of an "I" who wants or needs enlightenment collapses, and what remains is free of contraction and desire, enjoying life as a miracle of creation appearing out of nothing, and seeing through the delusions and foibles of the conventional mindset, including your own. Enlightenment is the condition of living in the moment from the pure awakened consciousness before it attaches itself to any desire or condition. It is relaxing into spontaneity and responding without division in a way that is open and free of conditioning, moving from the heart and a natural wisdom. It is that which sees through the veils of delusion about life, including our self-delusion. When kundalini awakens, you are in the initiating stage of this process, when deconstruction of the old way of seeing things has begun. You may have glimpses of vast new perspectives along the way. Keep going, until everything has settled and there is no one who cares if anything more is added, or has objections when ordinary life intervenes.

Does this mean I have special powers?

Not necessarily. Some people awaken an ability to heal, have precognitive abilities, or find themselves astral traveling (as if the energy body is going outside of the physical body to another space or time). Usually these phenomena pass as awakening deepens. Such things also happen for a few people without kundalini awakening. These experiences can be distracting by-products of awakening, and there is no great advantage to their pursuit. Most spiritual schools will tell you they can take you off the path to realization, because they bring the temptation of becoming a new identity that is more "spiritual" or "special" and you can get stuck in that for many more lifetimes. Some schools of training, however, are all about developing these capacities, and if that is your destiny, your heart's calling, you will probably go in that direction, as least until the impulse has burned away and lost its ability to intrigue you. After all, the game of walking on water, manifesting objects, precognition, levitating, and transmigrating is only another dimension of experience and has very little practical utility in your life.

When will the intensity stop?

When it gets around to it. If you follow the 10 basic guidelines it should become subtler, and if you allow the energy time to flow and do what it needs to do, it is less likely to disturb you at other more inconvenient times. No two people navigate this journey in exactly the same way. You can get used to having more intense energy, especially if you do what you need to do to be sure your body stays as healthy as possible and you avoid over-stimulating your nervous system.

What should I do when my body shakes involuntarily?

Lie down and let it play out whatever it is trying to release. If you let the energy move it will usually relax after a few minutes. Or if you cannot release it at the moment because you are driving or working, stop, and focus outside of yourself, on a distant tree or landscape, and take some calming breaths. Sit with a teacher who has gone beyond the energy, and soak in the peacefulness. Talk to the energy and ask it to take it easy for a while. Dance and move with the energy, or paint it on a large piece of butcher paper, expressing all that is coming up for you in the moment. Eat some protein and root vegetables. If this is a continual problem you cannot manage, get a physical and be sure your nervous system is in balance. Your hormones or adrenal glands may need some attention.

There are scary entities arising in my mind? What should I do?

If you have scary or demonic images coming to mind they are not real, but only manifestations of thoughts. You are not real, but only a compilation of your conditioning and tendencies living in a body-vehicle made of energy flows, so how can they be real? They are energetic forms that are symbolic, which doesn't mean they have no power, only that you give it to them by believing in them.

There are three explanations with which I am familiar that could explain why these images come to a few people. The first is that they represent frightening and repressed experiences and impulses that could not be adequately dealt with as children, so they come into the mind in a symbolic way. Dismemberment, torture, and other stories express very dark and extremely painful feelings that are challenging to face and deal with. In such cases it can be useful to have some therapeutic intervention to deal with these old distressing events. Some may even be the residual of the events of a past life, arising now to be faced and made impotent. You can't carry old fears or stories into awakening. Consciousness wants you to see through everything that is unreal.

Another reason for these demonic forces is that you may have invited them into consciousness in this or a previous life by playing with dark or black magic. There are satanic cults and a few shamanic systems that deliberately generate destructive energies, and if some part of you has called these into play then in a sense they belong to you, and you must face them and tell them you no longer have any use for them in your life, and insist that they depart. You may also call upon beings of light, love or wisdom to intercede on these dimensional planes and help you to be rid of the darkness. If you have a positive spiritual guide or image that has heartfelt meaning for you, bring them into your mind and imagine them supporting your work in eliminating the distraction of these energies.

A third condition that may cause negative images and fearful stories to arise is as a reaction to drugs. I have consulted with people who have used LSD who suffer a later reactivation of hallucinations and images that are frightening, especially if there is either trauma or conditioned fear of the devil in their background. This generally passes in time, as the impact of the drug experience wears off.

What is the meaning of my vision?

There is no need in a spiritual process to understand the meaning of a vision. If insight arises, you may find this interesting and it can be comforting, and sometimes a vision is a way of the subconscious imaging an important movement or transition in your life; but if not, it may be just as valuable, because it arose from the unconscious to unfold something new in the psyche. What you need to "know" will be given to you in right timing. Unlike psychotherapy, which helps you make your life work better by examining the deep unconscious memories of history, spiritual awakening has no interest in activities of the mind for self-understanding. The movement is to release dependence on thought and mind, disengaging consciousness from its enmeshment with the personal life, so that you can directly experience your Self, which is the Whole, unlimited, vastness, the One. Knowledge and understanding in a spiritual process is cellular, deeper than thought, something akin to an intuitive revelation that you have no control over and cannot call up on demand. It can be felt as a kinesthetic knowing, or a heart opening that spontaneously reveals what is true and arises separately from the efforts of mind.

What is the meaning of the synchronicities?

Again, there is no need to understand synchronicity. It simply happens for many people during certain stages of awakening, and can come and go as rapidly as sun and rain. When it occurs it feels like a confirmation. You have a thought of someone and the phone rings, and it is she or he calling you. You walk in a book store and just the book you need falls off of a shelf. You dream about a bird, and one flies into your house the next day. You turn on the television and there is exactly the information you need. It appears that at certain times the universe cooperates with what we need, and shows us there is a greater presence in our life that we can rely on. Many people think of synchronicity as an affirmation of their choice or direction taken at the moment. It is one of the little blessings or miracles of human experience.

What's the energy/vibration/scraping/wiring going on in my head?

It seems to be a reorganization of how the brain works, perhaps a new way that energy is distributed as the prana intensifies after kundalini arises or following a shattering insight that wipes out the old way of connecting the dots of our thinking. Many people experience this after an awakening of energy, or following a great change of perspective after an awakening of consciousness. It can last a short while, or continue for months. If it causes you headaches, try a meditation practice in which you bring awareness down into the chest, parallel to the heart but to the right of the sternum, (where the spiritual heart is said to reside, or the source of consciousness). Just rest your focus there. Or bring attention and breath down into the belly. Energy follows attention, so move your attention somewhere else. Be sure you are eating healthy and adequately, avoiding intoxicants, bringing balance into your life and not indulging in toxic thoughts and negativity. Talk to the energy as if it is a goddess, asking her to take it easy or take some time off. This may all sound trite in the midst of dramatic crisis, but they are methods that help. Sometimes cranial-sacral work, or acupressure can also help to calm and redistribute energy that gets too intense in one area of the body. Some people find hugging trees, or walking in the sand or ocean, calms things down.

Why is my life changing so much?

This is a process that ends the old patterns of your life, challenging anything that is not authentic, or no longer useful. It is like taking a house down in order to remodel it, bringing in more light and more flexibility, and letting life flow in and out of it more gracefully. If you have asked for a spiritual awakening, this is the response. Many people do not understand the deep and profound shifts that are inherit in true spiritual realization, for it causes you to be "born anew", as the Bible said. This is not the old little "me" who gets to become someone better. Rather it is falling into the root of what you always were and always will be, the indestructible, universal and loving spaciousness that is the ground of being, the kingdom within. This that becomes awake to itself then uses the life and the body in a new way that is not familiar to the ego, no longer driven by the ego desires and demands. Instead there is a gentle leaning, or an inner message, or a happiness to serve in whatever arises in the life. A new clarity and wisdom becomes available.

When we see what we truly are, we can no longer cling to the remnants of what we thought we were, because they are seen to be as insubstantial as the image in a broken mirror. Freedom is the capacity to move from this new place, this changed life, and discover the wonders and quiet happiness it can bring. When kundalini awakens its intention is to bring you fully into this new home. It offers paradoxically both stillness and radiant living, emptiness and fullness, compassion and love.

APPENDIX

Books About Spiritual Awakening & Kundalini
(Annotated Bibliography by Bonnie Greenwell)

(This is a partial listing of the many books available which include some discussion of kundalini, or present a good introduction to yoga or spiritual awakening for people seeking ways to support their own kundalini awakening.)

Adyashanti. (2008) **The End of Your World: Uncensored Straight Talk on the Nature of Enlightenment**. Boulder, CO. (Offers clarity on the kinds of experiences that often follow an awakening, and the passage from awakening to liberation.)

Adyashanti. (2003). **My Secret is Silence**. Los Gatos, CA. Open Gate Sangha. (Brief sayings and poetry by a remarkable awakened teacher that touch the heart, unsettle the mind and bring insights related to spiritual awakening.)

Adyashanti. (2006). **Emptiness Dancing.** Sounds True, Boulder, CO (A collection of dharma talks by Adyashanti, describing the major themes of his teachings.)

Aurobindo, S. (1971). **Letters on Yoga**. (4 parts) Pondicherry: Sri Aurobindo Ashram. (Discussions about spiritual development, problems and stages of spiritual practice, and transformation of physical and subtle bodies. Esoteric, lengthy, but interesting & readable for those interested in yoga philosophy.)

Bentov, I. (1977). **Stalking the Wild Pendulum: On the Mechanics of Consciousness.** New York: Bantam.

(Introduces idea of physio-kundalini complex, and explores scientific approach to consciousness.)

Caplan, Mariana. Halfway Up the Mountain: The Error of Premature Claims to Enlightenment. (An excellent compilation of teachings from several traditions warning of the delusion of enlightenment which follows intense spiritual experiences.)

Cousins, Gabriel. (1986). **Spiritual Nutrition and the Rainbow Diet.** Boulder: Cassandra Press. (Good discussion of Kundalini and subtle body theory, sharing some of his personal experience, and introducing dietary approach to supporting spiritual processes.)

Edwards, L. (1996). **The Soul's Journey: Guidance from the Goddess Within** (Av. from Dr. Edwards at 45 Lake Shore Dr., Putnam Valley, NY 10579.) (A personal account of visionary and awakening experiences, and his approach to establishing a relationship with the "divine presence".)

Freke, T. & Gandy, P. (2002). **Jesus and the Lost Goddess: The Secret Teachings of the Original Christians**. (Great book with incredible research about early Jewish and Christian Gnosticism, which is the best analogy I have seen that shows how Jewish and Christian mystical practices originally led to self-realization or enlightenment in the same way it is described in Hindu and Buddhist traditions. Nothing here about kundalini, but tremendous clarity about self-realization, and how it happened that the Christian churches no longer recognize or support it.)

Goel, B.S. (1985). **Third Eye and Kundalini**. India: Third Eye Foundation. (Hard to find; a detailed autobiographical description of the awakening of an

Indian intellectual who studied Freud and Marx. Shows clearly emotional problems, self-doubts, and other problems that can accompany awakening.)

Greenwell, B. (1995). Energies of Transformation: A Guide to the Kundalini Process. Shakti River Press. Ashland, OR (A comprehensive overview of Eastern and Western views of Kundalini, including 23 case histories, descriptions of seven categories of symptoms, and guidelines for assisting someone in this process. Currently out of print). Contact www.kundainiguide.com for updates)

Greenwell, B. (2014) The Awakening Guide, Shakti River Press, Ashland, OR. (a companion to The Kundalini Guide, focused on the awakening stages that follow.) Available late summer 2014 on Amazon

Grof, S. and Grof, C. (1990). Spiritual Emergency: When Personal Transformation Becomes a Crisis. Los Angeles, CA. Tarcher. (An anthology of many experiences. A good overview of a varieties of spiritual emergency including information on NDE, psychic opening, Shamanic openings, kundalini.)

Grof, C. (1990). The Stormy Search for the Self. Los Angeles, CA. Tarcher. (Information similar to the above, but includes Christina's personal experiences and information on addiction and spiritual emergence, and general guidelines for working with spiritual emergence.)

Gupta, S. (1971). The Laksmi Tantra -- A Pancaratra text. Leiden, Netherlands: E.J.Brill. (Available at CA. Inst. of Integral Studies, S.F. CA., library; scriptures describing Kundalini as a goddess, and the methods and outcomes of a relationship with her.)

Hari Dass, B. (1981). **Ashtanga Yoga Primer.** Santa Cruz: Sri Rama. (Basic introduction to the practices of Ashtanga or eight-limbed yoga, including use of yogic locks, pranayama and asana. A how-to book; no specific references to Kundalini.)

Harrigan, J. (2000). **Kundalini Vidya: A Comprehensive System for Understanding and Guiding Spiritual Development.** (A detailed description of kundalini science including the chakras, nadis and movement of kundalini energy, based on the kundalini tradition in Tamil.) Available through Patanjali Kundalini Yoga Care at www.kundalinicare.com)

Harris, B. and Bascom, L. (1990). **Full Circle: The Near-death Experience and Beyond.** New York: Simon & Shuster. (An enjoyable story of Harris's personal story of NDE and the impact it had on her life, with a scientific commentary.)

Irving, Darrel (1995). **Serpent of Fire: A Modern View of Kundalini**. York Beach, ME: Weiser. (A basic discussion of the myth and reality of Kundalini awakening, including details of the author's experiences, two interviews with Gopi Krishna, and comparisons of Kundalini with bipolar illness.)

Jayakar, P. (1986). **Krishnamurti: A Biography.** San Francisco: Harper & Row. (Describes in some detail Krishnamurti's kundalini experiences.)

Joy, B. (1979). **Joy's way: A Map for the Transformational Journey**. Los Angeles J.P. Tarcher. (Joy, a physician and healer, describes his kundalini experiences and theories regarding subtle body energy.)

Judith, A. (1996). **Eastern Body Western Mind;**

Psychology and the Chakra System. Berkeley: Celestial Arts. (An extensive exploration of the chakra system as a seven-leveled philosophical model of the universe, and of chakras as the transmitters of life force energy. Offers a detailed description of the relationship of psychological forces to the chakras.)

Kalweit, H. (1988). **Dreamtime & Inner Space: The World of the Shaman.** Boston: Shambala. (If you think your kundalini experience has echos of Shamanic experience this is an excellent overview of the inner world of the shaman, with several descriptions that sound much like kundalini phenomena, and helpful perspectives on near-death, out-of-body and other altered state experiences.)

Kason, Y. (1996). **A Farther Shore: How Near-death and Other Extraordinary Experiences Can Change Ordinary Lives**. San Francisco : Harper Collins (An excellent, thorough description of the Kundalini process, using the model proposed by Gopi Krishna, and expanded by Dr. Kason, who is a physician specializing in work with people who have had spiritual experiences. Many vignettes and stories of people in various spiritual processes with some emphasis on the awakening of spiritual, psychic and creative abilities.)

Karanjia, R. K. (1977). **Kundalini Yoga.** New York: Kundalini Research Foundation. (Good descriptions and information regarding Kundalini)

Keating, Thomas (2006) **Open Mind, Open Heart** Bloomsbury Academic Press (An excellent introduction to meditation from a Christian perspective, including many of the conditions that arise).

Kennett, J., and MacPhillamy, Rev. D. (1977). **How to**

176

Grow a Lotus Blossom. Mt. Shasta, CA.: Shasta Abbey.
(Describes Kennett's personal experiences during her
third stage kensho, or spiritual awakening, with many
visionary experiences. A radical book to be offered from a
Zen Buddhist monk -- also see The Wild,Wild Goose, a
book about her initial awakening experiences.)

Kennett, J. (1979). **The Book of Life.** Mt. Shasta, CA.:
Shasta Abbey. (Describes theories regarding bodywork
based on ancient Anma massage to help people with
energies awakened due to meditation.)

Kalsa, Newberg, Rhada, Wilbur, Selby et al (2009)
Kundalini Rising: Exploring the Energy of Awakening,
Boulder: Sounds True. (A modern anthology of various
perspectives of kundalini awakening, with a chapter by
Dr. Greenwell.)

Krishna, G. (1993 rev. by Leslie Shepherd). **Living With
Kundalini.** Boston: Shambala. (His detailed
autobiography, a version of Kundalini: The Evolutionary
Energy in Man, updated and expanded, describing a wide
range of difficult experiences and ultimate transformation
with Kundalini, and providing much theory.)

Lad, V. (1984). **Ayurveda: The Science of Self-healing.**
New Mexico: Lotus. (Describes Indian medicine as taught
for thousands of years in relationship to diet, food
categories, exercises and constitutional aspects which
balance the elements and the body to attune it
physically, emotionally and spiritually.)

Lumiere-Wins, John and Lynn Marie. (2000). **The
Awakening West: Evidence of a Spreading
Enlightenment**. Clear Visions Publications, Oakland.
(Interviews with 15 contemporary spiritual teachers,
primary of the Advaita or Non-dual traditions, with

insights into their personal stories and experiences of awakening.)

Malik, Arjan. (1991 & 1994). **Kundalini and Meditation.** Published by Ajay Kumar Jain, Manohar Publications, 2/6/ Ansari Rd. Daryaganj, New Delhi 110 002. (A nice story of a classic awakening with a teacher in India.)

Maharshi, Sri Ramana. (1989).**Talks With Sri Ramana Maharshi.** Published by Venkataraman, Sri Ramansramam, Tiruvannamalai. (An excellent collection of talks given by a great modern Advaita teacher and sage of India, who is credited with bringing the teachings of non-dualism back into the forefront of India teachings. Many modern non-dual teachers have come from his lineage, and this book is one of several that give clear and understandable teachings on the nature of Self and Self-inquiry.)

Mishra, R. (1959). **Fundamentals of Yoga.** New York: Lancer. (Excellent introduction to yoga theory and practice.)

Mishra, R. (1963). **Yoga Sutras: The Textbook of Yoga Psychology.** New York: Anchor. (Excellent interpretation of Patanjali's Yoga Sutras.)

Mookerjee, A. (1983). **Kundalini, the Arousal of the Inner Energy**. New York: Destiny. (Easy to read, skims a broad range of information on chakras, subtle energies, tantra and kundalini.)

Motoyama, H. (1981). **Theories of the Chakras: Bridge to Higher Consciousness**. Wheaton, Ill.: Theosophical Publishing House. (Describes his personal experience with kundalini, and relates specific changes to the

movement of kundalini through the chakras; suggests
practices for opening each chakra.)

Moss, Richard (1986). **The Black Butterfly**. Berkeley,
Ca. Celestial Arts. (A Western physician and healer
describes his experiences of awakening and his work
leading seminars.)

Muktananda, S. (1978). **Play of Consciousness.**
Ganeshpuri, India: Gurudev Siddha Peeth.
(Autobiography describing his experiences, and
presenting clearly the significance of the guru in Indian
spiritual practices, and many experiences of visions,
energy and consciousness.)

Muktananda, S. (1979). **Kundalini: The Secret of Life.**
South Fallsburg, N.Y.: SYDA Foundation. (Small book
with descriptions of the positive aspects of kundalini.)

Narayanananda, S. (1950). **The Primal Power in Man or
the Kundalini Shakti.** Gylling, Denmark: N.U.Yoga
Trust & Ashrama. (Includes discussion of some problems
of kundalini & recommendations.)

Paulson. G. (1995). **Kundalini and the Chakras: A
Practical Manual.** Llewellyn Pub. (A good introduction
with an esoteric slant and emphasis on practices for the
chakras from a woman with a Christian background,
esoteric "New Age" language, and experience with people
who have activated kundalini energy in her training
programs.)

Pradhan, V.G. (1969). **Jnaneshwari: A Song-sermon on
the Bhagavadgita** (Vols. 1-2). London: Blackie and Son.
(Inspiring poetic interpretation of the Gita, a classic
Indian scripture. This is the only version of the Gita (I
know of) in which kundalini is specifically described and

discussed.)

Prasad, R. (1969). **Nature's Finer Forces (rev. ed.).**
London: H.P.B. Press. (Complex and specific description
of prana, the subtle body, and the science of breath
according to Indian scriptures.)

Radha, S. (1978). **Kundalini Yoga for the West.**
Boulder, CO.: Shambala. (Presents Radha's views of the
chakras, with psychological issues and practices for
transformation.)

Radha, S. (1981). **Diary of a Woman's Search.** Canada:
Timeless. (Autobiography describing her spiritual
experience in India, with emphasis on her psychological
struggles and yoga practices.)

Radhakrishnan, S. and Moore, C. (1957). **A Sourcebook
in Indian Philosophy.** Princeton, N. J.: Princeton
University. (Good history of Indian thought and scripture
without discussion of kundalini.)

Ring, Kenneth (1992). **The Omega Project: Near Death
Experiences. UFO Encounters and Mind at Large.** New
York: William Morrow. (An outstanding scientific study of
the presenting conditions and early childhood patterns of
people who report NDE and UFO experiences and report
some of the phenomena related to kundalini awakening.)

Rishabhchand (1953). **The Integral Yoga of Sri
Aurobindo. (2 vol.)** Pondicherry: Sri Aurobindo Ashram.
(Excellent and understandable introduction to teachings
of yoga as interpreted by Aurobindo; discusses specific
problems and solutions regarding the spiritual life.)

Sannella, L. (1987). **The Kundalini Experience.** Lower
Lake, CA. Integral Publishing. (Important book for

Western therapists written by physician, comparing kundalini with psychosis and speculating on the reasons for awakening. Includes many symptoms and case histories.)

Saraswati, S. (1984). <u>**Kundalini Tantra.**</u> Mungar: India: publ. by Sri G.K. Kejriwal at Bihar school of Yoga. (This is an excellent overview of the kundalini tradition and philosophy, including experiences and practices which awaken and nurture the process.)

Saraswati, S. (1967 or 1982). **Taming the Kundalini** Published by Bihar School of Yoga, India. (Letters from the Swami to his students with lots of guidance about their process.)

Satprem. (1970). **Sri Aurobindo or the Adventure of Consciousness.** Pondicherry: Sri Aurobindo Ashram Trust. (Good overview of the Aurobindo teachings).

Scott, M. (1983). **Kundalini in the Physical World.** London, Routledge & Kegan Paul. (Views of a scholar who has studied tantra and yoga and describes kundalini as an earth energy, relating it to the energy flows of the entire planet.)

Selby, John (1992). **Kundalini Awakening: A Gentle Guide to Chakra Activation and Spiritual Growth.** Bantam Books. (Has simple exercises and is a gentle guide, as it says it is. This book is a very simplified approach to the experience.)

Singh, J. (Trans.) (1979a). **Siva Sutras: The Yoga of Supreme Identity.** Delhi: Motilal Banarsidass. (Classical scripture describing higher consciousness.)

Sivananda, S. (1935). **Kundalini Yoga.** Himalayas:

Divine Life Society. (Classical discussion of the practice of Kundalini Yoga, including descriptions of the subtle body, and specific yoga practices.)

Sivananda, S. (1969). **Spiritual Experiences (Amrita anubhava).** Himalayas, India: Divine Life Society. (Discusses some of the ecstasies and problems of spiritual aspirants)

Some, Malidoma (1994). **Of Water and Spirit**. Penguin Books. (A remarkable story of a spiritual teacher trained in the African Shamanic tradition. Kidnapped in Africa, and taken to a Jesuit mission school, and raised for 15 years by Europeans, he then returned to his home and underwent shamanic initiation. He later moved to the USA.

St. Romain, P. (1991). **Kundalini Energy and Christian Spirituality.** New York: Crossroads. (A Christian perspective of the awakening process, told by the experiencer.)

Teasdale, W. (1999). **The Mystic Heart: Discovering a Universal Spirituality in the World's Religions**. New World Library, Novato. (A synthesis of the issues related to spiritual awakening and mysticism and the "transforming presence of the divine in all traditions.")

Tirtha, S. (1948). **Devatma Shakti: (Kundalini) Divine Power.** India: Yoga Shri Peeth Trust. (Excellent overview describing kundalini by a respected authority. A thorough and understandable presentation of subtle body system).

Tweedie, I. (1986). **Daughter of Fire.** Grass Valley: Blue Dolphin. (Autobiography describing kundalini experiences within a guru relationship in India.)

Venkatesananda, Swami. (1976). **The Supreme Yoga: A New Translation of Yoga Vasistha (2 volumes).** Divine Life Society, Himalyas, India. (This is a wonderful Advaita scripture from India for those ready and able to study the foundational Truths of Self-Realization. These teachings describe the non-dual perspective of creation, existence and the nature of Self and consciousness. Vasistha was a great ancient rishi and sage of India.)

White, J. (1979). **Kundalini, Evolution and Enlightenment.** New York: Anchor. (A collection of essays by scholars and yogis describing aspects of the Kundalini process.)

Whitfield, B. Spiritual awakenings: Insights of the Near-death Experience and Other Doorways to the Soul. Deerfield Beach, Fl: Health Comm. (Tells a remarkable spiritual awakening story, and describes a range of awakening experiences including NDE, kundalini, and psychic awakenings, along with hints on how to hold on through the power of these processes, and the need for unconditional love.)

Made in United States
Cleveland, OH
21 June 2025

17877624R00105